Best of Bridge
Done in One

Best of Bridge

Done in One

Perfect Recipes in
One Pot, Pan or Skillet

Robert
ROSE

For complete cataloguing information, see page 216.

Disclaimer
The recipes in this book have been carefully tested by our kitchen and our tasters. To the best of our knowledge, they are safe and nutritious for ordinary use and users. For those people with food or other allergies, or who have special food requirements or health issues, please read the suggested contents of each recipe carefully and determine whether or not they may create a problem for you. All recipes are used at the risk of the consumer.

We cannot be responsible for any hazards, loss or damage that may occur as a result of any recipe use.

For those with special needs, allergies, requirements or health problems, in the event of any doubt, please contact your medical adviser prior to the use of any recipe.

DESIGN AND PRODUCTION: Kevin Cockburn/PageWave Graphics Inc.
EDITOR: Kathleen Fraser
INDEXER: Gillian Watts
PHOTOGRAPHY: Jonathan Bielaski
PROP STYLIST: Mecayla Slaviero
ASSISTANT FOOD STYLIST: Kate Mlodzik
ICONS: © Getty Images

COVER IMAGE: Skillet Lasagna (page 168)

We acknowledge the support of the Government of Canada.

Canadä

Published by Robert Rose Inc.
120 Eglinton Avenue East, Suite 800, Toronto, Ontario, Canada M4P 1E2
Tel: (416) 322-6552 Fax: (416) 322-6936
www.robertrose.ca

Printed and bound in China

1 2 3 4 5 6 7 8 9 ESP 31 30 29 28 27 26 25 24 23

CONTENTS

~

INTRODUCTION

No matter what kind of day you've had, no matter where you've been before you step into your kitchen, at work, home or school, at the end of the day, you need to get dinner on the table. We know the value of cooking smarter. That's where *Done in One* steps in to help streamline meal preparation. The recipes in this book are based on food being cooked in one vessel — be that a skillet, sheet pan, stock pot, casserole dish, Dutch oven, Instant Pot or slow cooker.

The recipes have also been developed to use minimal equipment, which mean less clean up and is also good news for those with compact kitchens. There's no need to use every bowl and spatula to make one dish! We appreciate the value of time when it comes to meal preparation and washing up afterward. We say yes to using the same pan to cook different components of a dish and yes to lining baking sheets to skip the scrubbing. Wiping out a bowl or a pan for the next step is one way to keep the cooking going and reduce the clean-up time.

Sheet pans can be so versatile in cooking all kinds of meals, from breakfast to dessert. These satisfying meals are a cinch to clean up: Sheet-Pan Breakfast Bagels and Sheet-Pan Beef and Mushroom Fajitas. We like to use large, rimmed baking sheets that will accommodate a full meal; however, smaller half-sheet pans are handy for smaller items, including small roasts that don't have a lot of drippings. Roasting pans that have higher sides can also be used as sheet pans in a pinch, so rejoice if you haven't used yours in a while.

Using a single skillet to cook a meal is clean-up happiness. Our Creamy Mushroom and Lentil Orzo, Vegetable Beef Curry and Skillet Lasagne are delicious meals that your family will love. Using large nonstick skillets helps reduce the amount of oil you need to use and they really clean up well, but having a regular skillet will help with browning; we recommend having both if possible. This includes cast-iron skillets, which can be a bit heavy but they do create a delicious crust on steaks and retain heat that helps in cooking — not to mention the extra iron that you get in your diet!

Pots of various sizes, from a larger soup pot or Dutch oven (which is any pot with a lid) to a small saucepan, are wonderful for soups and stews. You can drain your pasta then return the same pot to the stove to finish up the sauce. So many recipes need one pot only — once you get started on this path, you will wonder why you didn't do it before!

You'll be happy to know that we've included an Instant Pot version of our famous Hamburger Soup. Forty years since it was featured in the first Best of Bridge cookbook, it was time to put a new spin on this beloved, classic soup that so many people have told us they grew up enjoying. Instant Pots have been winning fans for years and slow cookers are still holding strong, so we made sure to include plenty of recipes your family will enjoy for these classic one-pot vessels.

Many of the recipes include icons so you can quickly identify, for example, if the recipe cooks in 30 minutes or less, is perfect for making ahead or uses five ingredients or fewer. The book is also filled with tips for substitutions, how-tos and ideas on how to riff on the recipe. Recipes aren't written in stone and we encourage you to adapt the recipes to best meet the taste preferences in your household. You'll find many vegetarian and gluten-free recipes in this book, as family needs can evolve, and we want everyone to celebrate in cooking and eating well together. Check out our full list of icons so you can start planning your meals together.

In keeping with the Best of Bridge style, easy-to-find ingredients are available that produce flavorful results. We know you love to use grocery store shortcuts as much as we do, so we have included ingredients such as frozen puff pastry, canned beans, frozen vegetables and canned fish to speed up meal preparation. We hope that these recipes inspire you to do more with less mess, so you can spend more time eating and enjoying and less time washing up afterward! Although we would never turn down the opportunity to wash and dry dishes alongside each other when that means catching up on the day's gossip together.

As always, we look forward to hearing your stories from the kitchen and about the recipes you've tried, so get in touch. Send us an email, post your photos and tag us on Instagram @BestofBridge and on Facebook. We look forward to fewer pots and pans and more food and fun with family and friends!

All our best,
Sylvia and Emily

GUIDE TO RECIPE ICONS

 MAKE AHEAD: Recipes that can be prepared in advance, including recipes that can be made ahead in stages to cook later

 5 INGREDIENTS OR FEWER: Recipes that use five main ingredients or fewer, not including water, oils, salt and black pepper

 30 MINUTES OR LESS: Recipes that can be prepared from start to finish in 30 minutes or less

 SHEET PAN: Recipes that are cooked on a sheet pan and baked in the oven

 ONE SKILLET/POT MEAL: Recipes that require only one pot or one skillet to cook

 VEGETARIAN: Recipe ingredients do not include meat or fish products but can include dairy, eggs and honey.

 GLUTEN FREE: Recipe ingredients do not contain any gluten, which is protein found in wheat and other grains such as barley and rye. (Please read labels for ingredients when cooking at home to ensure no wheat products have been used.)

BREAKFAST & BRUNCH

~

STRAWBERRY BREAKFAST SMOOTHIES

SERVES 2 · (30) · 🗑

Strawberries and bananas taste great together. The oats and chia seeds make the smoothies creamy and satisfying.

〜〜〜〜〜〜〜〜〜〜〜〜〜〜〜〜〜〜〜〜〜〜〜〜〜

¼ cup (60 mL) quick oats

1 tbsp (15 mL) chia seeds

2 cups (500 mL) frozen strawberries

1 cup (250 mL) plain yogurt

1 cup (250 mL) milk

1 ripe banana

2 tbsp (30 mL) strawberry jam

1 In a blender, place oats and chia seeds; blend until finely ground. Add strawberries, yogurt, milk, banana and jam; blend until smooth. Makes 4 cups (1 L).

TIP
For a vegan version, substitute plant based dairy alternatives for the yogurt and milk.

MAKE AHEAD
Make and freeze in freezer-safe jars; thaw overnight in the fridge. Freeze for up to 1 month.

We think we should work at a smoothie shop. We feel like we'd blend in.

CINNAMON-GLAZED PUMPKIN SHEET-PAN PANCAKES

MAKES 12 PANCAKES · · ·

We love hosting breakfast at our homes and this easy sheet-pan recipe makes it that much easier. These pancakes freeze well, so you might like to make a double batch to have on hand.

2 1/4 cups (550 mL) all-purpose flour

3 tbsp (45 mL) granulated sugar

1 1/2 tsp (7 mL) ground cinnamon

1 tsp (5 mL) baking powder

1 tsp (5 mL) baking soda

1/2 tsp (2 mL) ground ginger

1/2 tsp (2 mL) grated nutmeg

1/2 tsp (2 mL) salt

1/4 tsp (1 mL) ground cloves

1 1/4 cups (300 mL) milk

1/2 cup (125 mL) plain Greek yogurt

1/2 cup (125 mL) pumpkin purée

2 large eggs

3 tbsp (45 mL) canola oil

1/3 cup (75 mL) chopped walnuts or pecans

1 Preheat oven to 425°F (220°C). Line an 18- by 13-inch (45 by 33 cm) rimmed baking sheet with parchment paper and lightly spray with nonstick cooking spray; set aside.

2 In a large bowl, whisk together flour, sugar, cinnamon, baking powder, baking soda, ginger, nutmeg, salt and cloves. In a medium bowl, whisk together milk, yogurt, pumpkin, eggs and oil. Pour milk mixture over flour mixture and whisk until just combined but still slightly lumpy. Pour mixture onto prepared sheet and spread batter to completely fill baking sheet. Sprinkle walnuts on top. Bake 12 to 15 minutes or until a toothpick inserted in the middle come out clean.

3 In the meantime, prepare Cinnamon Glaze (see below). Cut pancake into pieces and drizzle with Cinnamon Glaze.

CINNAMON GLAZE

In a small bowl, combine 1 cup (250 mL) confectioners' (icing) sugar, 2 tbsp (30 mL) milk, 1 tbsp (15 mL) very soft butter, 1/2 tsp (2 mL) vanilla and 1/4 tsp (1 ml) ground cinnamon. Mix together until smooth.

SKILLET GRANOLA

SERVES 6 TO 8 ·

This quick-to-prepare small batch of granola is perfect
for breakfast and snacking. Toasting the oats in the
skillet gives the granola a deep nutty flavor.
This granola is also the perfect topping for our
Upside-Down Granola Rhubarb Cake on page 206.

2 cups (500 mL) large-
flake (old-fashioned)
rolled oats

1/4 cup (60 mL) sliced
almonds

1/4 cup (60 mL) sunflower
seeds

1/4 cup (60 mL)
unsweetened shredded
coconut

3 tbsp (45 mL) canola oil

2 tbsp (30 mL) maple syrup
or honey

2 tbsp (30 mL) packed
brown sugar

1/2 tsp (2 mL) ground
cinnamon

1/4 tsp (1 mL) freshly grated
nutmeg

Pinch salt

1/2 cup (125 mL) dried
cranberries (optional)

2 tbsp (30 mL) flax seeds
(optional)

1 In a large skillet, over medium-high heat, add oats
and cook for 3 minutes, stirring frequently until
fragrant and light brown. Reduce heat to medium
and add almonds, sunflower seeds, coconut, oil,
maple syrup, brown sugar, cinnamon, nutmeg and
salt. Cook 4 to 5 minutes, stirring occasionally;
reduce heat if the mixture browns too quickly.

2 Remove from heat and stir in cranberries and
flaxseed, if using; mix until evenly combined. Let
cool completely in pan, mixture will become crisp
as it cools. Transfer to an airtight container for up
to 1 month. Makes 3 cups (750 mL).

TIPS

Old-fashioned oats can be labeled as rolled oats
or large-flake oats.

To make this gluten-free, use gluten-free oats
instead of regular oats.

Substitute raisins, dried cherries or dried
blueberries for the cranberries.

MAKE AHEAD

Store granola in an airtight container and freeze
for up to 3 months.

BREAKFAST SKILLET

SERVES 2 TO 3 · · ·

Using all your favorites in this skillet breakfast will leave you satisfied and ready to take on your daily chores. This is a hearty morning meal but also perfect for brunch or a midday meal.

8 oz (250 g) sliced bacon, chopped

2 tbsp (30 mL) butter

2 potatoes, diced (about 12 oz/375 g total)

1/2 tsp (2 mL) dried thyme leaves (optional)

1/2 tsp (2 mL) each salt and black pepper, divided

1/3 cup (75 mL) sour cream

1/3 cup (75 mL) salsa

1 tbsp (15 mL) chopped fresh parsley or cilantro (optional)

2 large eggs

1/4 cup (60 mL) shredded sharp (old) Cheddar cheese

Pickled jalapeño pepper slices (optional)

1 Preheat oven to 400°F (200°C).

2 In a cast-iron skillet, cook bacon over medium-high heat for about 8 minutes or until crispy. Remove with a slotted spoon to a paper towel lined plate. Drain all but 2 tbsp (30 mL) of the bacon fat in skillet; add butter until melted.

3 Add potatoes, thyme and half each of the salt and pepper. Cook, stirring occasionally for about 10 minutes or until potatoes are golden and tender.

4 Meanwhile, in a small bowl, stir together sour cream, salsa and parsley, if using. Stir into potatoes along with bacon and stir to coat. Make two wells in the mixture, crack the eggs into them and sprinkle each with remaining salt and pepper. Place in oven and bake for about 6 minutes or until eggs are desired doneness.

5 Remove from oven and sprinkle with cheese and jalapeños, if using, to serve.

TIPS

Add 2 more eggs to easily serve 4 for breakfast.

If you don't have a cast-iron skillet, you can use a regular skillet that is oven safe for this recipe.

SHEET-PAN BREAKFAST BAGEL SANDWICHES

SERVES 4 · (30) · 🔲

We love how this classic breakfast is conveniently baked on just one sheet pan. If you need breakfast on the go, simply wrap the fresh baked sandwiches and head out the door.

4 large eggs

Everything bagel spice blend

4 bagels, split

Butter for spreading on bagels

4 thin slices smoked deli ham (about 6 oz/175 g)

4 slices sharp (old) Cheddar cheese (about 6 oz/175 g)

1 green onion, chopped

1 tomato, thinly sliced

1 avocado, thinly sliced

1 Preheat oven to 425°F (220°C). Line one-third of a rimmed sheet pan with foil, fold edges up to create a lip all around to help keep the eggs together while they bake. Spray foil with nonstick cooking spray. Gently crack the eggs onto the foil, then sprinkle with a bit of the spice blend. Bake for 3 minutes.

2 Meanwhile, butter the bagels. After the eggs have baked for 3 minutes, remove pan from oven and place bagels on pan, butter side up on the empty side of the sheet pan. Place a slice of ham on 4 of the bagel halves, followed by a slice of cheese and a sprinkle of green onion. Return pan to oven and bake another 2 to 3 minutes or until eggs are cooked to desired doneness and cheese is melted.

3 To assemble, place one egg on the ham and bagel half, along with a slice of tomato and avocado. Top with the other half of the bagel. Serve hot.

TIP
Instead of Cheddar cheese slices, try with mozzarella, Havarti or Jalapeño Jack cheese.

PARTY-SIZE POTATO ROSTI

MAKES 12 TO 16 SERVINGS · · ·

Potato pancakes are always a hit for brunch but can be time consuming when you have to make them individually or there might not be enough! This baking sheet–size version will have you ready to serve 12 to 16 people. Or cut it smaller for bite-size appetizers!

5 lb (2.5 kg) yellow-fleshed potatoes, peeled

1 small, sweet onion, finely chopped

2 garlic cloves, minced

2½ cups (625 mL) shredded Gruyère or Jarlsberg cheese

3 green onions, thinly sliced

3 tbsp (45 mL) canola oil

2 tsp (10 mL) chopped fresh thyme

½ tsp (2 mL) salt

½ tsp (2 mL) black pepper

Sour cream or French onion dip (optional)

Smoked salmon or trout (optional)

1 Preheat oven to 400°F (200°C). Line a large baking sheet with parchment paper.

2 Using a box grater or the shredding blade in a food processor, grate potatoes and place in large bowl. Toss with onion and garlic. Squeeze potato mixture and discard liquid. Return to bowl and stir in cheese, green onions, oil, thyme, salt and pepper until evenly distributed.

3 Press potato mixture evenly into pan. Roast for 50 to 60 minutes or until deep golden brown and crisp all over.

4 Let cool slightly and, using pizza cutter or chef's knife, cut into desired pieces. Top each piece with sour cream and salmon, if using, to serve.

TIPS

You can grate the onion and garlic too instead of chopping.

If you have leftovers, you can easily heat them up in the oven or in a skillet to add to another breakfast or brunch.

BAKED HAM AND EGG CUPS

SERVES 6 ·

Everything bakes together in one little cup to serve for breakfast or brunch. Add some toast or an English muffin to round it out. These can be made ahead and warmed up for an easy on-the-go breakfast or to tuck into someone's lunch.

12 slices Black Forest ham (about 12 oz/375 g total)

1½ cups (375 mL) shredded sharp (old) white Cheddar cheese, divided

⅓ cup (75 mL) herbed cream cheese

Half a small red or orange bell pepper, diced

12 large eggs

Salt and black pepper

2 tbsp (30 mL) chopped fresh chives or green onion

1 Preheat oven to 400°F (200°C). Lightly spray a 12-cup muffin tin with nonstick cooking spray.

2 Line each muffin tin with a slice of ham to shape the cup. Sprinkle about 1 tbsp (15 mL) of the Cheddar cheese onto the bottom of each.

3 In a small bowl, stir together herbed cream cheese and pepper. Dollop a small amount into each cup. Crack eggs into each cup and sprinkle with some salt and pepper. Bake for about 15 minutes or until whites are set and yolks are slightly soft. (You can leave them longer for a firmer yolk.) Remove from oven and sprinkle with remaining cheese and chives to serve.

FLORENTINE VARIATION
Substitute 1 cup (250 mL) baby spinach, chopped, for the bell pepper

PROSCIUTTO VARIATION
Substitute thinly sliced prosciutto for sliced Black Forest ham. (You will need about 24 slices as they are thinner and smaller than the ham slices).

TIP
Make these breakfast cups up to 4 days ahead. Keep them refrigerated and warm them in the oven or microwave for anyone who needs a great breakfast.

CHICKEN CHORIZO BREAKFAST PATTIES

SERVES 4 ·

Plenty of basic pantry spices go into this recipe to get that delicious Mexican-style chorizo flavor we love.

SPICE MIXTURE

1 tbsp (15 mL) smoked paprika

1 tbsp (15 mL) garlic powder

1 tbsp (15 mL) chili powder

2 tsp (10 mL) packed brown sugar

1 tsp (5 mL) dried oregano

1 tsp (5 mL) onion powder

$\frac{1}{2}$ tsp (2 mL) ground cumin

$\frac{1}{2}$ tsp (2 mL) hot pepper flakes

$\frac{1}{2}$ tsp (2 mL) salt

$\frac{1}{2}$ tsp (2 mL) black pepper

$\frac{1}{4}$ tsp (1 mL) ground cinnamon

$\frac{1}{8}$ tsp (0.5 mL) ground cloves

PATTIES

1 lb (500 g) ground chicken or turkey

$\frac{1}{2}$ cup (125 mL) finely chopped red bell pepper

$\frac{1}{4}$ cup (60 mL) dry bread crumbs

2 tbsp (30 mL) red wine or cider vinegar

Canola oil for frying

1 In a medium bowl, combine the spice mixture. Add chicken, red pepper, bread crumbs and vinegar; mix until well combined. Cover and refrigerate at least 4 hours or overnight. Shape into 8 patties about $\frac{1}{2}$ inch (1 cm) thick.

2 In a skillet, heat a little oil over medium-high heat. Add patties and cook 3 to 4 minutes per side until golden or until patties are cooked through and reach an internal temperature of 165°F (74°C).

TIPS

These patties are perfect to serve alongside hash browns, in an English muffin or wrapped in a tortilla with salsa, cheese and scrambled eggs.

The spice mixture can be made several days ahead. Store in a covered container until ready to use.

Cooked patties can be refrigerated for up to 3 days or frozen for up to 2 months.

MAPLE CARROT DONUTS

SERVES 12 · 🌱 · ⏱ 30

These light and fluffy donuts are a wonderful baked treat to share with friends. Be sure to set some aside before the kids get their hands on them — they will disappear! Just ask Emily's friend Donna, whose kids ask for this on repeat.

DONUTS

2 cups (500 mL) all-purpose flour

1/2 tsp (2 mL) baking powder

1/2 tsp (2 mL) baking soda

1/2 tsp (2 mL) ground cinnamon

1/2 tsp (2 mL) salt

1 cup (250 mL) sour cream

2 large eggs

1/3 cup (75 mL) canola oil

3 tbsp (45 mL) maple syrup

3/4 cup (175 mL) granulated sugar

3/4 cup (175 mL) finely grated carrot

GLAZE

1 cup (250 mL) confectioners' (icing) sugar

2 tbsp (30 mL) maple syrup (approx.)

1 DONUTS: Preheat oven to 350°F (180°C). Lightly spray donut pan with nonstick cooking spray; set aside.

2 In a bowl, whisk together flour, baking powder, baking soda, cinnamon and salt.

3 In a large bowl, whisk together sour cream, eggs, oil and maple syrup. Add sugar and whisk until combined. Add flour mixture and carrot; stir until batter is smooth and no flour remains.

4 Scrape batter into a piping bag or use a resealable bag and cut the corner. Pipe into prepared pan and bake for about 10 minutes or until tester comes out clean. Let cool in pan 5 minutes, then remove from pan to completely cool on a rack.

5 GLAZE: Sift confectioners' sugar into a bowl and whisk in maple syrup until smooth and runny, adding up to 1 tbsp (15 mL) more if necessary.

6 Dip each donut into glaze and place on cooling rack set over baking sheet. Enjoy immediately or let stand until glaze sets before serving.

VARIATION

Use mini donut pans instead of full-size donut pans. Recipe will make about 24 mini donuts.

If you don't have a donut pan, you can use a muffin tin.

EARL GREY TEA BREAD

SERVES 8 TO 10 ·

Earl Grey tea is typically a blend of black tea and bergamot oil, which comes from a type of citrus fruit. We've added orange zest and a hint of lavender to give this loaf a fragrant citrus and floral note.

2 large eggs

1 cup (250 mL) granulated sugar

3/4 cup (175 mL) canola oil

1 cup (250 mL) full-fat sour cream

2 tbsp (45 mL) Earl Grey tea leaves from about 6 tea bags

2 tsp (10 mL) vanilla extract

1 tsp (5 mL) grated orange zest

1/4 tsp (1 mL) crushed dried lavender (optional)

2 cups (500 mL) all-purpose flour

1 tsp (5 mL) baking powder

1/2 tsp (2 mL) salt

1/2 tsp (2 mL) baking soda

1 Preheat oven to 350°F (180°C). Spray a 9- by 5-inch (23 by 12.5 cm) loaf pan with nonstick cooking spray or line with parchment paper.

2 In a large bowl, whisk together eggs, sugar and oil until very well blended. Whisk in sour cream, tea leaves, vanilla, orange zest and lavender, if using. In another bowl, whisk together flour, baking powder, salt and baking soda. Add the flour mixture into the wet ingredients and stir until just combined.

3 Pour batter into prepared pan and bake for about 1 hour or until a tester inserted in the center comes out clean. Leave to cool in pan for 10 minutes, then turn loaf out onto a wire rack to cool completely.

TIPS

If desired, substitute gluten-free flour for the all-purpose flour.

Cover and store bread at room temperature for 1 day or in the refrigerator for up to 4 days.

REFRIGERATOR RAISIN BRAN MUFFINS

MAKES 20 SMALL MUFFINS · ·

Many people don't make muffins in the morning because of time constraints, but when you have the batter already in the fridge, all you need do is scoop and bake. You'll have instant fresh muffins in about 20 minutes, perfect for on-the-go morning snacks. Add your favorite dried fruit to the mix if desired.

3 cups (750 mL) bran flakes cereal

1 cup (250 mL) wheat bran

2 cups (500 mL) milk

3/4 cup (175 mL) packed light brown sugar

1/2 cup (125 mL) canola oil

2 large eggs

1 tsp (5 mL) grated orange zest (optional)

1 1/2 cups (375 mL) whole wheat flour

2 tsp (10mL) baking powder

1 tsp (5 mL) ground cinnamon (optional)

1/2 tsp (2 mL) baking soda

1/2 tsp (2 mL) salt

1 cup (250 mL) raisins

1 In a large bowl, stir together cereal, wheat bran, milk, brown sugar, oil, eggs and orange zest, if using.

2 Stir in flour, baking powder, cinnamon, if using, baking soda and salt until well moistened.

3 Add raisins and stir to combine. Cover and refrigerate for at least 6 hours or up to 2 days.

4 Preheat oven to 400°F (200°C). Lightly spray muffin tins with nonstick cooking spray.

5 Gently stir batter before scooping into desired number of prepared tins. Bake for 15 to 20 minutes or until golden and firm to the touch.

TIPS

You can substitute dried chopped apples, dried cranberries or currants for the raisins.

Bake only as many muffins as you need over the course of the three days so you will always have a fresh batch of muffins.

APPETIZERS

~

APPLE ONION CHUTNEY

MAKES 1¼ CUPS (300 ML) · · · ·

Tangy and sweet, this fresh-tasting chutney adds a wonderful contrast to old Cheddars and strong aged cheeses and adds zip to creamy rich ones such as Brie and Camembert. Emily's friend Kate served it up for family and friends who wanted the recipe — here you go, everyone!

2 tbsp (30 mL) butter

1 small, sweet onion, chopped

1 large apple, peeled, cored and diced

¼ cup (60 mL) cider vinegar

3 tbsp (45 mL) packed light brown sugar

2 tsp (10 mL) yellow mustard seeds

¼ tsp (1 mL) ground cinnamon

1 In a skillet, melt butter over medium-high heat and cook onion, stirring for about 8 minutes or until starting to become golden. Reduce heat to medium, add apple and cook for about 5 minutes or until beginning to soften. Increase heat to medium-high and add vinegar, brown sugar, mustard seeds and cinnamon and cook, stirring for 3 minutes or until thickened.

TIPS

Substitute canola oil for the butter to make this chutney vegan and use it on your favorite vegan cheeses.

Sweet onion varieties include Walla Walla and Vidalia.

Cover and refrigerate for up to 2 weeks. Be sure to stir well before serving. This is best served at room temperature.

CRAB-STUFFED TOMATOES

MAKES 10 TO 12 · ·

These little appetizers will add color to your holiday table.
The prepared dip adds plenty of flavor to the crab
and speeds your prep time.

1 package (1 lb/500 g)
cocktail tomatoes

1/2 cup (125 mL) canned
crabmeat, drained

1/2 cup (125 mL) artichoke
and asiago dip

2 tbsp (25 mL) chopped
fresh parsley

2 tbsp (30 mL) grated
Parmesan cheese

5 black olives, pitted and
quartered

Freshly ground black
pepper (optional)

1 Cut top stem off tomatoes to expose pulp. Using
small spoon, scoop out pulp and seeds and discard.
Place tomatoes cut side down on paper towel lined
plate for 5 minutes to drain. Trim bottom slightly to
help sit up straight, if necessary.

2 In a bowl, combine crabmeat, dip, parsley and
cheese. Use a small spoon to fill tomatoes. Place
on platter and top with olives and pepper, if using,
to serve.

HOT TOMATO VARIATION

Place filled tomatoes on parchment paper lined
baking sheet and bake in 400°F (200°C) oven
for 5 minutes or until filling is heated through.

STUFFED MUSHROOM VARIATION

Add 2 tbsp (30 mL) seasoned dry bread crumbs to
filling. Remove stems from 1 package (14 oz/397 g)
stuffing mushrooms. Use a small spoon to create
a little hole in mushrooms. Fill with filling and bake
on parchment paper lined baking sheet in 400°F
(200°C) oven for 15 minutes or until golden brown
and mushrooms are tender.

MANGO SALAD MARTINI CUPS

SERVES 6 TO 8 ·  ·

The freshness of a tart mango salad makes your mouth happy and serving it up in a martini glass makes it a statement! No martini glasses, no problem — it's easily served in lettuce cups. This makes a great appetizer for any cocktail party.

1 large mango, ripe but firm

¼ cup (60 mL) finely diced red onion

2 tbsp (30 mL) finely diced red bell pepper

2 garlic cloves, minced

2 tbsp (30 mL) lime juice

1 tbsp (15 mL) granulated sugar

1 tbsp (15 mL) fish sauce

Asian chili paste (optional)

¼ cup (60 mL) chopped toasted cashews

Fresh cilantro leaves

1 Peel mango. Slice mango into thin strips along flat side of pit to remove fruit. Finely dice mango and place in a bowl. Add red onion, red pepper, garlic, lime juice, sugar, fish sauce and Asian chili paste to taste, if using. Stir to combine.

2 Spoon mango salad into each martini glass. Sprinkle with cashews and garnish each with cilantro.

TIP

Mango salad can be made ahead. Store in the refrigerator in an airtight container for up to 2 days. Sprinkle with cashews and cilantro just before serving.

IT takes TWO to Mango!

ROASTED TOMATO AND RED PEPPER BRUSCHETTA

SERVES 4

We enjoy a variation on a classic. This savory appetizer — a delicious way to enjoy fresh tomatoes and basil — includes capers, smoked paprika and a little heat. Don't skip the step of rubbing the bread with garlic, as it adds so much flavor!

4 cups (1 L) grape tomatoes (2 pints)

1 yellow or red bell pepper, cut into 1/2-inch (1 cm) pieces

2 tbsp (30 mL) extra virgin olive oil, divided

2 tsp (10 mL) capers, finely chopped

1 tsp (5 mL) red wine vinegar

1 tsp (5 mL) dried oregano

1/2 tsp (2 mL) smoked paprika

1/2 tsp (2 mL) hot pepper flakes

Salt and black pepper

8 slices ciabatta (about 3/4 inch/2 cm thick)

2 garlic cloves, halved

1/4 cup (60 mL) fresh basil leaves, sliced into thin strips

1 Position one oven rack in the middle and another about 5 inches (12.5 cm) from the top of the oven. Preheat oven to 400°F (200°C).

2 Place tomatoes and pepper on a rimmed baking sheet, drizzle with 1 tbsp (15 mL) oil and toss to coat. Place baking sheet on the middle oven rack and bake 25 to 30 minutes or until tomatoes and pepper soften. Transfer to a bowl; let cool 5 minutes, then add remaining oil, capers, vinegar, oregano, paprika and hot pepper flakes. Season with salt and pepper to taste.

3 Meanwhile, turn oven to broil. Toast bread on top oven rack until lightly charred, then rub the garlic halves on the bread. Just before serving, sprinkle tomato mixture with basil. Serve warm or at room temperature with toasted bread.

TIPS

Sourdough would also be a tasty bread choice.

Balsamic vinegar can be substituted for the red wine vinegar.

THAI CURRY CORN FRITTERS

SERVES 4 ·  · ·

You'll love our take on crispy corn fritters inspired by the popular Thai street food, Tod Man Khao Pod. The fritters are a perfect finger food to serve at your next get-together.

2 tsp (10 mL) Thai red curry paste

2 tsp (10 mL) fish sauce

1 large egg

2½ cups (625 mL) frozen corn kernels, thawed and drained

½ cup (125 mL) rice flour

¼ cup (60 mL) finely chopped Thai basil

2 tbsp (30 mL) corn meal

2 tbsp (30 mL) finely chopped red bell pepper

Oil for frying

Sweet chili sauce for dipping

1 In a medium bowl, stir together curry paste and fish sauce until combined. Beat in egg; then stir in corn, rice flour, basil, corn meal and red pepper.

2 In a heavy pot or deep skillet, heat ½ inch (2 cm) oil over medium heat. Drop the batter by tablespoonful (15 mL) into the oil. Fry fritters for 2 minutes until light golden brown, then flip over and fry another 2 minutes. Transfer to a paper towel lined baking sheet to drain excess oil. Serve hot with sweet chili sauce.

TIPS

Rice flour can often be found in the international aisle or the gluten-free aisle of the grocery store. Be sure to use regular rice flour and not the sweet or glutinous varieties.

You can also use fresh or canned corn kernels in this recipe.

Sweet basil can be substituted for Thai basil, but it will not have that subtle anise flavor.

To make this vegetarian, use vegan fish sauce.

CRISPY RICE PAPER BITES

SERVES 18 ·

Crispy on the outside, chewy and crunchy on the inside,
these two-bite appetizers are filled with Thai-inspired flavor.

1 tsp (5 mL) canola oil

1 cup (250 mL) finely chopped cooked chicken

1 cup (250 mL) finely shredded cabbage

1 small carrot, finely grated

2 green onions, finely chopped

2 garlic cloves, minced

2 tbsp (30 mL) finely chopped fresh cilantro

1 tbsp (15 mL) fish sauce

2 tsp (10 mL) lime juice

1 tsp (5 mL) finely grated fresh ginger

1 tsp (5 mL) soy sauce

1 tsp (5 mL) granulated sugar

1 tsp (5 mL) sesame oil

1 tsp (5 mL) Sriracha

2 tsp (10 mL) cornstarch

18 round rice paper wrappers (8 inches/20 cm)

Canola oil for frying

Prepared sweet chili sauce for dipping

Sliced cucumbers

1 In a large nonstick skillet, heat oil over medium-high heat. Add chicken, cabbage, carrot, green onions, garlic, cilantro, fish sauce, lime juice, ginger, soy sauce, sugar, sesame oil and Sriracha; stir to combine, then stir in cornstarch. Cook 2 minutes, stirring occasionally. Set aside to cool slightly, about 10 minutes.

2 In a pie plate or shallow dish filled with room-temperature water, soak one rice paper wrapper for a few seconds until just pliable. (The wrapper will continue to soften.) Place on a clean, slightly damp flat work surface to help keep the wrapper from sticking to the surface. Place a tablespoon (15 mL) of filling onto the center of the wrapper. Fold to enclose filling to create a small package. Repeat with remaining ingredients.

3 Using the same skillet, rinse and wipe clean. Heat a bit of oil in pan over medium-high heat; add bites seam side down, about $1/2$ inch (1 cm) apart. If necessary, fry in batches, as the bites tend to stick to each other if they touch. Cook about 3 minutes per side, until crispy and lightly golden, adding more oil as needed. Serve with sweet chili dipping sauce and cucumbers.

TIP

You can substitute turkey for the chicken.

MAKE AHEAD

The filling can be prepared 1 day ahead; cover and refrigerate until ready to assemble.

MISO-GLAZED BRUSSELS SPROUTS WITH BACON

SERVES 4 ·

Sylvia and her family enjoy this Brussels sprouts recipe as a favorite appetizer item. We love the caramelized flavor, the salty crunch of the bacon and the crispy edges of the Brussels sprouts.

4 slices bacon, cut into ½-inch (1 cm) pieces

1 lb (500 g) Brussels sprouts, trimmed, cut in half lengthwise

½ tsp (2 mL) black pepper

¼ tsp (1 mL) salt

3 garlic cloves, skin removed and roughly chopped

1 tbsp (15 mL) white or yellow miso

1 tbsp (15 mL) cider vinegar

1 tbsp (15 mL) maple syrup or honey

1 tsp (5 mL) toasted sesame seeds

1 Preheat oven to 425°F (220°C).

2 In a large cast-iron skillet or heavy ovenproof skillet, over medium-high heat, cook bacon pieces until they begin to crisp, stirring occasionally, about 10 minutes. Transfer bacon to a bowl, leaving bacon drippings in the skillet. Add Brussels sprouts, pepper and salt; toss to combine. Cook for 2 minutes without stirring to sear the sprouts. Then add garlic, give the sprouts a stir and cook another 2 minutes.

3 Transfer skillet to oven and bake for 5 minutes, then stir, add bacon and bake another 5 minutes or until sprouts are crispy.

4 Meanwhile, in a small bowl, whisk together miso, vinegar and maple syrup.

5 Remove skillet from oven, drizzle with half of the miso mixture and toss to combine. Serve the remaining sauce for dipping.

TIPS

When buying Brussels sprouts, choose ones that that are bright green, compact and similar in size for even cooking. The smaller sprouts tend to have a sweeter flavor.

White miso is mild in flavor and is also called shiro miso or sweet miso.

REUBEN PARTY DIP

MAKES 2 CUPS (500 ML) · ·

We turned the Reuben sandwich, a favorite for many, into an awesome hot party dip! Dip each rye bread cube into the dip to enjoy the perfect balance of flavors in a whole new way. This one will be an entertaining hit.

½ cup (125 mL) mayonnaise

½ cup (125 mL) Thousand Island salad dressing

4 oz (125 g) thinly sliced corned beef, finely chopped

⅓ cup (75 mL) sauerkraut

1 small garlic clove, minced

1 cup (250 mL) shredded Swiss cheese

1 loaf rye bread, cubed

1 In a saucepan, stir together mayonnaise, salad dressing, corned beef, sauerkraut and garlic until combined. Place over medium-low heat and stir in Swiss cheese. Cook, stirring occasionally, for about 10 minutes or until cheese is melted and dip is hot.

2 Serve with bread.

TIPS

If you have a fondue pot, keep the dip warm and be sure the flame is low.

You can also keep this warm using a small slow cooker for dipping into.

Add a few extras, such as pickles and mustard, for the perfect sandwich dip experience.

A friend of ours wanted to make a Reuben sandwich but he couldn't find the right bread...
You could say his plans went a-rye.

SALADS

BASHED CUCUMBER SALAD

SERVES 6

Bashing the cucumber creates rough edges and helps it absorb the flavor of the dressing. This is a perfect make-ahead salad; the longer it sits, the more flavor gets into the cucumber. Enjoy it alongside your favorite grilled chicken, fish or steak.

SALAD

12 mini cucumbers

2 tsp (10 mL) salt

1 tsp (5 mL) granulated sugar

1 tbsp (15 mL) toasted sesame seeds

Chopped fresh cilantro

Chili oil (optional)

SESAME GINGER DRESSING

3 tbsp (45 mL) rice vinegar

2 garlic cloves, rasped

1 tsp (5 mL) grated fresh ginger

1 tbsp (15 mL) soy sauce

1 tbsp (15 mL) sesame oil

1 SALAD: Half cucumbers lengthwise. Place cucumbers in batches onto a cutting board and gently smash them with your hands or a mallet to crack the skin and give them an uneven look. Place cucumbers in a colander and sprinkle with the salt and sugar; let stand in colander for 20 minutes.

2 SESAME GINGER DRESSING: Meanwhile, whisk together vinegar, garlic, ginger, soy sauce and sesame oil; set aside.

3 Toss drained cucumbers with dressing and sprinkle with sesame seeds, cilantro and chili oil, if using, to serve.

TIPS

Emily's friend Shan suggests if you don't have chili oil, use hot pepper flakes instead. Sprinkle them on earlier so the flavor sets in better.

Cover and refrigerate for up to 3 days.

CUCUMBER TOMATO SALAD WITH ZA'ATAR

SERVES 6 · · ·

Middle Eastern spice za'atar adds a bright bold flavor
to this refreshing salad. Feel free to swap other available
fresh greens for the arugula.

1 English cucumber,
chopped

2 cups (500 mL) grape
tomatoes

1 yellow bell pepper,
chopped

1 cup (250 mL) chopped
fresh parsley

1/2 small red onion, thinly
sliced

2 tbsp (30 mL) extra virgin
olive oil

1 tbsp (15 mL) lemon juice

2 tbsp (30 mL) za'atar
spice mix

1 cup (250 mL) lightly
packed arugula

1 cup (250 mL) broken pita
chips

1/2 cup (125 mL) crumbled
feta cheese

Salt and black pepper

1 In a large bowl, combine cucumber, tomatoes, yellow
pepper, parsley, red onion, olive oil, lemon juice and
spice mix. Just before serving, toss in arugula, pita
chips and feta. Season with salt and pepper to taste.

TIP
Za'atar spice mix is a delicious blend of oregano,
marjoram, cumin, coriander, sumac and sesame
seeds.

MAKE AHEAD
Chop vegetables ahead of time; store in the
refrigerator until ready to assemble salad.

FIVE-BEAN SALAD

SERVES 8 ·

Bean salads have been classic summer fare forever.
But it doesn't mean you can't change it and make it better.

½ cup (125 mL) dried green or brown lentils

8 oz (250 g) green beans, trimmed and chopped into bite-size pieces

½ cup (125 mL) extra virgin olive oil, divided

2 celery stalks, finely chopped

1 red bell pepper, diced

1 carrot, shredded

¼ cup (60 mL) sherry or red wine vinegar

3 tbsp (45 mL) basil pesto or sun-dried tomato pesto

1 tsp (5 mL) Dijon mustard

¾ tsp (3 mL) salt

¼ tsp (1 mL) black pepper

1 can (19 oz/540 mL) chickpeas, drained and rinsed

1 can (19 oz/540 mL) red kidney beans, drained and rinsed

1 can (19 oz/540 mL) black beans, drained and rinsed

¼ cup (60 mL) chopped fresh mint

¼ cup (60 mL) chopped fresh parsley

1 In a large saucepan of boiling water, cook lentils for 10 minutes. Add green beans and cook for about 7 minutes or until tender crisp. Drain and rinse under cold water; leave in colander.

2 Return saucepan to medium heat. Add 2 tbsp (30 mL) of the oil to saucepan and sauté celery, red pepper and carrot for 3 minutes to soften slightly. Remove from heat and stir in vinegar, pesto, mustard, salt and pepper. Add lentils and green beans, chickpeas, kidney beans and black beans, stirring to combine well. Add mint and parsley and stir to combine.

MAKE AHEAD

This salad can be made up to 2 days ahead and stored covered in the refrigerator.

TIP

Use your favorite canned beans in this salad. You can also try canned mixed beans for an even greater bean variety.

BEET, CITRUS AND PEAR SALAD

SERVES 6 · ·  ·

Loaded with crunch and texture made bright with a
white wine dressing, this refreshing and colorful salad
looks as beautiful as it tastes.

DRESSING

1/3 cup (75 mL) canola oil

2 tbsp (30 mL) white wine
vinegar

2 tsp (10 mL) Dijon mustard

2 tsp (10 mL) granulated
sugar

1/4 tsp (1 mL) each salt and
black pepper

1 garlic clove, minced

SALAD

6 cups (1.5 L) mixed salad
greens

1 medium beet, peeled and
coarsely grated or cut
into matchsticks

1 firm Bartlett pear, thinly
sliced

1 orange, peeled and
sliced into 1/4-inch
(0.5 cm) rounds

1/2 cup (125 mL) crumbled
goat cheese

1/2 cup (125 mL) roasted
sunflower seeds

1 DRESSING: In a small bowl or mason jar, whisk or
shake together oil, vinegar, mustard, sugar, salt,
pepper and garlic; set aside.

2 SALAD: Arrange the salad greens on a platter;
arrange beets and pear with orange on top, then
sprinkle with goat cheese and sunflower seeds.
Drizzle dressing over salad just before serving.

TIPS

The beet can also be spiralized or shredded in
a food processor.

The salad is delicious added to a grain bowl.

Refrigerate the dressing for up to 1 week.

ROAST TOMATO, BACON AND CORN SPINACH SALAD

SERVES 4 ·

Creamy dressing with sweet roasted tomatoes and corn marks the late summer harvest. Enjoy it with a crisp glass of white wine to celebrate the weekend.

SALAD

4 cobs of corn, shucked

4 cups (1 L) grape tomatoes

2 garlic cloves, minced

2 tbsp (30 mL) chopped fresh parsley

2 tbsp (30 mL) canola oil

1/4 tsp (1 mL) each salt and black pepper

1 container (5 oz/142 g) baby spinach

6 slices bacon, cooked and chopped

BUTTERMILK DRESSING

1/4 cup (60 mL) buttermilk

3 tbsp (45 mL) light mayonnaise

2 tbsp (30 mL) rice vinegar

1 tbsp (15 mL) chopped fresh basil or parsley

1/4 tsp (1 mL) each salt and black pepper

1 Preheat oven to 425°F (220°C). Line a baking sheet with parchment paper.

2 SALAD: Cut kernels from cobs of corn and combine with tomatoes, garlic and parsley on prepared baking sheet. Drizzle with oil, salt and pepper and toss to coat. Roast for about 20 minutes or until tomatoes are blistered; set aside.

3 BUTTERMILK DRESSING: In a small bowl, whisk together buttermilk, mayonnaise, rice vinegar, basil, salt and pepper.

3 Toss together roast tomatoes and corn with spinach and bacon and drizzle with dressing to serve.

FRESH COUSCOUS SALAD

SERVES 6 TO 8 · ·

This salad will surprise you every time. You don't need to cook the couscous before you start; after it sits for at least 4 hours, it is ready to be served. How's that for easy!

~~~~~~~~~~~~~~~~~~~~~~~~~~~~

1 cup (250 mL) canned diced tomatoes with juices

1/2 cup (125 mL) extra virgin olive oil

1/3 cup (75 mL) fresh lemon juice

1 tbsp (15 mL) dried oregano

1/4 tsp (1 mL) hot pepper flakes (optional)

1 1/2 cups (375 mL) instant couscous (uncooked)

1 1/2 cups (375 mL) grape tomatoes, halved

1 cup (250 mL) diced cucumber

Half each yellow and red bell pepper, diced

1/2 cup (125 mL) diced celery

1/3 cup (75 mL) chopped fresh basil

1/3 cup (75 mL) chopped fresh parsley

Salt and black pepper

Chopped fresh basil

1 In a large bowl, stir together tomatoes, oil, lemon juice, oregano and hot pepper flakes, if using. Stir in couscous, grape tomatoes, cucumber, yellow and red peppers, celery, basil and parsley. Cover and refrigerate for at least 4 hours or up to 24 hours.

2 Stir again; add salt and pepper to taste. Sprinkle with more chopped basil to add a fresh herb flavor when serving.

TIP

Salad can be covered and refrigerated for up to 3 days.

If you like, drizzle with a little extra virgin olive oil and add a sprinkle of fresh herbs when serving.

CALIFORNIA ROLL SALAD

SERVES 6 TO 8

Change it up and serve a favorite roll as a salad
for your next get together. Everyone can scoop some out
to enjoy and add the toppings they want to dress the
whole salad and have it ready for the potluck.

SUSHI RICE

2 cups (500 mL) sushi
 (Calrose) rice

2 cups (500 mL) water

1/3 cup (75 mL) rice vinegar

2 tbsp (30 mL) granulated
 sugar

3/4 tsp (3 mL) salt

1 small English cucumber,
 chopped

1/2 cup (125 mL) chopped
 green onions

SALAD TOPPINGS

8 oz (250 g) crabmeat

2 avocadoes, thinly sliced

3 sheets nori (seaweed),
 cut in strips

Pickled ginger

Sesame seeds

Soy sauce

Wasabi (optional)

1 SUSHI RICE: In a rice cooker or large saucepan, combine rice with water. Steam according to manufacturer's directions or bring to a simmer; cover saucepan and cook on low for about 25 minutes or until rice is firm, not soft. Meanwhile, whisk together vinegar, sugar and salt.

2 Slowly pour vinegar mixture over cooked rice and mix gently with a fork, trying not to mash grains of rice. Let cool. Stir in cucumber and green onion and spread onto serving platter.

3 SALAD TOPPINGS: Top with crab, avocado and nori. Garnish with pickled ginger and sesame seeds and serve with soy sauce and wasabi, if desired.

SPAGHETTI TUNA SALAD

SERVES 4 TO 6 · (:30) · 🍲

Change up your usual pasta salad for this fun new version with spaghetti! Zippy tuna and pantry ingredients create a fresh colorful salad perfect to serve anytime to family and friends.

1 package (1 lb/500 g) spaghetti pasta

1/3 cup (75 mL) extra virgin olive oil

2 garlic cloves, minced

1/4 cup (60 mL) basil pesto or sun-dried tomato pesto

1/4 cup (60 mL) white wine vinegar

2 cans (7 oz/198 g each) solid light tuna in oil (not drained)

2 cups (500 mL) grape tomatoes, halved

1/3 cup (75 mL) sliced pitted black sun-dried olives

1/2 cup (125 mL) chopped fresh basil or parsley

Freshly ground black pepper (optional)

1 In a large pot of boiling salted water, cook spaghetti for about 10 minutes or until al dente. Drain and rinse under cold water; set aside.

2 Return pot to medium-low heat and add oil and garlic. Cook, stirring for 2 minutes or until garlic is fragrant and light golden. Remove from heat and whisk in pesto and vinegar. Add tuna and spaghetti and toss to coat well. Add tomatoes, olives and basil and toss again before serving. Serve with freshly ground pepper, if desired.

TIP

If making the salad ahead, cover and refrigerate for up to 2 days. Be sure to drizzle a bit more oil over top and toss well before serving, if desired. Add some more chopped basil too for added freshness.

What game do fish like playing the most? Name that tuna!

SOUPS & SANDWICHES

INSTANT POT CAULIFLOWER CHEESE SOUP

SERVES 6 ·

The rustic texture of this soup comes in part from using the whole cauliflower, chopped leaves and stem included. Garnish with croutons and chopped chives.

2 tbsp (30 mL) canola oil

1 onion, diced

5 garlic cloves, minced

1 medium head cauliflower, chopped (about 2 lbs/1 kg)

2 celery stalks, diced

1 carrot, diced

1 tsp (5 mL) dried thyme

1 tsp (5 mL) salt

1/2 tsp (2 mL) black pepper

1/2 tsp (2 mL) hot pepper flakes

3 cups (750 mL) ready-to-use chicken broth

1 cup (250 mL) half-and-half (10%) cream

1 tbsp (15 mL) cornstarch

2 1/2 cups (625 mL) shredded Cheddar cheese, divided

1 In a 6-quart Instant Pot, select Sauté. Add oil and onion; cook 5 minutes, stirring occasionally. Add garlic and cook 30 seconds; then add cauliflower, celery, carrot, thyme, salt, pepper, hot pepper flakes and broth. Press Cancel and lock lid; set pressure release valve to Sealing. Press Manual Pressure Cook; set to High for 6 minutes. When cooking finishes; quick-release the steam by moving the pressure release valve to Venting. Press Cancel; open lid.

2 Select Sauté. In a small bowl, combine cream and cornstarch and stir into soup. Bring to a simmer, then press Cancel. Stir in 2 cups (500 mL) cheese. Ladle into bowls and top each with the remaining cheese.

TIPS
Use the cauliflower leaves and tender parts of the stem in this soup.

For a vegan version, substitute vegan cheese for the Cheddar cheese, coconut milk or soy cream for the cream and vegetable broth for the chicken broth.

MINESTRONE WITH PANCETTA AND WHITE BEANS

SERVES 4 TO 6 · ·

Whether you serve this chunky or decide to purée some of the soup, this flavorful vegetable powerhouse is perfect to serve with crusty bread. Minestrone typically has some sort of greens in it, so clean out the crisper for this one and make it your own!

2 tbsp (30 mL) canola oil

4 oz (125 g) diced pancetta

1 onion, chopped

1 large carrot, chopped

1 celery stalk, chopped

4 garlic cloves, minced

1 tsp (5 mL) chopped fresh rosemary or $\frac{1}{4}$ tsp (1 mL) dried

$\frac{1}{2}$ tsp (2 mL) hot pepper flakes

$\frac{1}{3}$ cup (75 mL) dry red wine

3 tbsp (45 mL) tomato paste

3 cups (750 mL) coleslaw mix

1 can (19 oz/540 mL) white kidney beans, drained and rinsed

5 cups (1.25 L) ready-to-use chicken broth

$\frac{1}{2}$ tsp (2 mL) salt

2 tbsp (30 mL) chopped fresh Italian parsley

1 In a soup pot, heat oil over medium-high heat and cook pancetta, onion, carrot, celery, garlic, rosemary and hot pepper flakes for about 5 minutes or until golden.

2 Add wine and tomato paste; cook, stirring until wine has almost all evaporated. Add coleslaw mix and white beans and stir to coat. Add broth and salt and bring to a boil. Cover and simmer for about 20 minutes or until coleslaw is very tender.

3 Use an immersion blender or pour half of the soup into a blender or food processor and purée until smooth. Return to soup pot and reheat until steaming.

4 Ladle soup into shallow soup bowls and sprinkle with parsley.

TIP

If you have cabbage in the fridge that needs to be used up, simply shred it and use it in place of the coleslaw mix.

HEARTY TUSCAN RIBOLLITA SOUP

SERVES 6 ·

This soup really hits the spot on a cold winter's night. Depending on where you eat it in Italy, the soup is either thickened with bread or simply poured over bread for a hearty bowlful.

1 tbsp (15 mL) canola oil

1 onion, chopped

4 garlic cloves, minced

1 carrot, chopped

1 celery stalk, thinly sliced

1 tsp (5 mL) dried thyme leaves

1/4 tsp (1 mL) hot pepper flakes

1 yellow-fleshed potato, peeled and diced

4 cups (1 L) ready-to-use vegetable or chicken broth

1 can (28 oz/796 mL) diced tomatoes

6 cups (1.5 L) shredded Swiss chard

1 can (19 oz/540 mL) white kidney beans, drained and rinsed

1/4 tsp (1 mL) each salt and black pepper

6 slices toasted Italian bread

1/4 cup (60 mL) grated Parmesan cheese

1 In a large pot, heat oil over medium heat and cook onion, garlic, carrot, celery, thyme and hot pepper flakes for about 5 minutes or until softened. Add potato and stir to combine. Add broth and tomatoes and bring to boil. Reduce heat and simmer for 15 minutes.

2 Add Swiss chard, kidney beans, salt and pepper and cook, stirring occasionally for about 10 minutes or until chard is tender.

3 Place bread in bottom of six soup bowls. Ladle soup over top of bread and sprinkle with cheese.

GREENS OPTIONS

You can substitute savoy cabbage, rapini or spinach for the Swiss chard.

CORN, BEAN AND SAUSAGE SOUP

SERVES 6 · ⏲ 30 · 🍲

This filling soup is perfect for enjoying fresh
summer corn and tomatoes when they're in season.
Serve with crusty bread on the side.

1 tbsp (15 mL) canola oil

12 oz (375 g) mild Italian
sausages

1 onion, chopped

4 cups (1 L) ready to use
chicken broth

2 cups (500 mL) fresh corn
kernels

1 can (19 oz/540 mL) navy
beans, undrained

2 medium tomatoes,
chopped

1/2 tsp (2 mL) each salt and
black pepper

1/2 tsp (2 mL) hot pepper
flakes

1 green onion, chopped

1 In a large pot, heat oil over medium-high heat and
fry sausages until cooked through, about 8 minutes.
Remove from pot, let cool 5 minutes, then cut into
1/2-inch (0.5 cm) pieces. Meanwhile, in the same
pot, over medium-high heat, add onion and cook
5 minutes, stirring occasionally. Add broth, scraping
up any brown bits from the bottom of the pot. Add
sausages, corn, beans, tomatoes, salt, pepper and
hot pepper flakes; bring to a boil then reduce heat
to medium. Cover and cook 7 minutes.

2 Remove from heat, stir in green onions and serve.

TIPS

The canned bean liquid helps to thicken the soup.
The salt level can vary between brands, so be sure
to taste and season just before serving.

Frozen corn kernels can be substituted for fresh
corn kernels.

KIMCHI SOUP

SERVES 6

This classic flavorful Korean soup is known as Kimchi Jjigae. Made of salted and fermented cabbage and seasonings, Kimchi provides a lot of complex flavors. Enjoy a steaming bowl of this delicious comforting soup which is traditionally served with hot cooked rice.

1 tbsp (15 mL) canola oil

1 onion, thinly sliced

1 lb (500 g) ground pork

4 garlic cloves, minced

1 tbsp (15 mL) finely grated fresh ginger

4 cups (1 L) ready-to-use chicken broth

2 cups (500 mL) kimchi, coarsely chopped

1 tbsp (15 mL) garlic chili paste or gochujang

1 tsp (5 mL) granulated sugar

1 tsp (5 mL) sesame oil

1 package (1 lb/500 g) medium-firm tofu, cut into 1/4-inch (0.5 cm) slices

2 stalks green onion, chopped

1 In a large pot, heat oil over medium-high heat. Add onion and cook for about 5 minutes, stirring occasionally until onions begin to brown and soften. Add pork, garlic and ginger and cook 5 minutes, stirring to break up pork into pieces. Add broth, scraping up any browned bits from the bottom of the pot. Add kimchi, garlic chili paste and sugar. Bring to a boil, cover and reduce heat to medium; simmer for 10 minutes.

2 Remove lid and stir in sesame oil, then gently stir in tofu. Cover and let simmer 10 minutes. Ladle into bowls and sprinkle green onion on top.

TIPS

You can also use firm tofu in this recipe.

Kimchi is available in jars and can be found in the refrigerated sections of the produce and health food aisles.

MAKE AHEAD

Refrigerate the soup in an airtight container for up to 4 days.

INSTANT POT BEST OF BRIDGE HAMBURGER SOUP

SERVES 10 ·

You'll love this version of our classic beloved — can we say famous? — hamburger soup! The Instant Pot cuts the cooking time so you can enjoy this wonderful bowl of goodness in about half an hour. It makes a big batch, perfect for sharing and for freezing. The original recipe can be found in the first Best of Bridge cookbook, published in 1975. It's the red book, if you know the books by the cover color.

1 tbsp (15 mL) canola oil

1 medium onion, chopped

1½ lbs (750 g) lean ground beef

4 medium carrots, chopped

3 celery stalks, chopped

½ cup (125 mL) pearl or pot barley

1 can (28 oz/796 mL) diced tomatoes

3½ cups (875 mL) ready-to-use beef broth

1½ cups (375 mL) tomato sauce

2 tbsp (30 mL) soy sauce

1 tbsp (15 mL) granulated sugar

1 tbsp (15 mL) cornstarch

½ tsp (2 mL) dried thyme

1 bay leaf

Salt and black pepper

1 In a 6-quart Instant Pot, select Sauté. Add oil and onion; cook 2 minutes, stirring occasionally. Add beef and sauté 5 minutes or until meat is browned and onions are softened, stirring occasionally and breaking it up with a spoon. Add carrots, celery, barley, tomatoes, broth, tomato sauce, soy sauce, sugar, cornstarch, thyme and bay leaf; stir to combine.

2 Press Cancel and lock lid; set pressure release valve to Sealing. Press Manual Pressure Cook; set to High for 15 minutes. (It takes about 10 minutes to come to pressure.)

3 When cooking finishes; quick-release the steam by moving the pressure release valve to Venting. Press Cancel; open lid and discard bay leaf. Season to taste with salt and pepper.

TIP
Refrigerate leftovers in an airtight container for up to 3 days. Freeze for up to 2 months.

MAKE AHEAD
Chop veggies the day before, cover and refrigerate until ready to cook.

PALWASHA'S AFGHAN CHICKEN SOUP

SERVES 6

Sylvia spent an afternoon learning how to make this Afghan soup, called Soup Morgh Wa Tarkari, from Palwasha and her daughter Shahira and friends. No measurements were specified, just plenty of visual and verbal estimates. The minor language barrier could not stop the laughter or the joy found in learning and sharing food from the heart.

8 cups (2 L) water

4 chicken bouillon cubes

4 boneless skinless chicken thighs

1 large onion, finely chopped

3 medium carrots, diced

3 garlic cloves, finely chopped

2 cups (500 mL) green peas

1½ tsp (7 mL) salt

1 tsp (5 mL) ground coriander

½ tsp (2 mL) ground turmeric

¼ tsp (1 mL) black pepper

1 cup (250 mL) lightly packed cilantro, finely chopped

¼ cup (60 mL) cornstarch

½ tsp (2 mL) vinegar

Soy sauce

Ketchup

1 In a 6-quart Instant Pot, add water and bouillon cubes, select Sauté and bring to a boil. Add chicken, onion, carrots, garlic, peas, salt, coriander, turmeric and pepper. Press Cancel and lock lid; set pressure release valve to Sealing. Press Manual Pressure Cook; set to High for 10 minutes.

2 When cooking is finished; quick-release the steam by moving the pressure valve to Venting. Press Cancel; open pot, select Sauté. Remove chicken from pot and shred; return to pot along with cilantro.

3 In a small bowl, stir together ½ cup (125 mL) water, vinegar and cornstarch; stir into soup. Bring to a simmer, cooking until soup thickens slightly, about 3 minutes. Press Cancel.

4 Serve drizzled with a little soy sauce and ketchup.

MAKE AHEAD
Refrigerate the soup in an airtight container for up to 4 days.

PAELLA SOUP

SERVES 6

Enjoy this simple flavorful soup version inspired
by the traditional Spanish rice dish paella.

1 tbsp (15 mL) canola oil

1 onion, chopped

4 oz (125 g) air-dried
chorizo sausage, thinly
sliced

1/2 cup (125 mL) dry white
wine

1/2 lb (250 g) boneless,
skinless chicken thighs,
cut into 3/4-inch (2 cm)
cubes

4 garlic cloves, minced

2 celery stalks, diced

1 yellow or red bell pepper,
chopped

2 tbsp (30 mL) tomato
paste

2 tsp (10 mL) smoked
paprika

2 tsp (10 mL) dried oregano

1 tsp (5 mL) salt

6 cups (1.5 L) ready-to-use
chicken broth

1 lb (500 g) medium-size
shrimp, peeled and
deveined

1 cup (250 mL) frozen
peas, thawed

2 tbsp (30 mL) chopped
fresh parsley

Lemon wedges

1 In a large pot, heat oil over medium-high heat.
Add onions and chorizo; cook 5 minutes, stirring
occasionally. Add wine; cook, stirring for
30 seconds, scraping up any brown bits from the
bottom of the pot. Add chicken and garlic, cook
1 minute, stirring occasionally. Stir in celery, bell
pepper, tomato paste, smoked paprika, oregano,
salt and broth. Bring to a boil, then cover and
reduce heat to medium. Simmer 10 minutes, then
stir in shrimp and peas. Cover, cook 3 minutes
or until shrimp are cooked through.

2 Ladle into bowls and sprinkle with parsley and serve
with lemon wedges on the side.

TIP

Chorizo sausage is available either fresh or dried.
For this recipe, be sure to use an air-dried, semi-
dried or dry-cured chorizo variety. Look for chorizo
in the meat or deli department of the grocery store.

Serve with hot cooked rice or crusty rolls.

MAKE AHEAD

Refrigerate the soup in an airtight container for up
to 4 days.

HOT AND SOUR SHRIMP SOUP

SERVES 4 TO 6 · ·

Try a spin on this restaurant favorite at home. Keep a bag of shrimp in the freezer to have it at the ready for this yummy soup.

6 cups (1.5 L) ready-to-use vegetable or chicken broth

1 shallot, thinly sliced

2 tsp (10 mL) minced fresh ginger

2 small garlic cloves, minced

1½ cups (375 mL) thinly sliced oyster mushrooms

1 cup (250 mL) diced firm tofu

1 can (7 oz/198 g) sliced bamboo shoots, drained

¼ cup (60 mL) rice vinegar

3 tbsp (45 mL) soy sauce

½ tsp (2 mL) hot pepper flakes

¼ cup (60 mL) cornstarch

¼ cup (60 mL) water

12 oz (375 g) large raw shrimp, peeled and deveined

1 large egg, beaten

Chopped green onions

1 In a soup pot, bring broth, shallot, ginger and garlic to a simmer. Stir in mushrooms, tofu and bamboo shoots and return to a simmer.

2 In a bowl, whisk together rice vinegar, soy sauce and hot pepper flakes. Stir into the soup. In same bowl, whisk together cornstarch and water. Stir into soup and return to a simmer until starting to thicken. Stir in shrimp and simmer gently for 3 minutes.

3 Gently drizzle the egg into the soup while stirring, then simmer for about 2 minutes or until soup is thickened and egg is set.

4 Ladle into bowls and sprinkle with green onions to serve.

TIPS

For a spicier version, increase the hot pepper flakes to 1 tsp (5 mL).

If oyster mushrooms are unavailable, you can substitute cremini mushrooms.

EASY NO-PEEL CLASSIC EGG SALAD SANDWICHES

SERVES 3 ·

Classic egg salad gets a new spin with a different way of preparing the eggs — they cook in a loaf pan that's set in a water bath. This no-peel method of hard-cooking eggs has been made extremely popular on social media, and it works!

6 large eggs, room temperature

3 tbsp (45 mL) mayonnaise

2 tbsp (30 mL) finely chopped celery

2 tbsp (30 mL) chopped green or red onion

2 tbsp (30 mL) chopped fresh dill

1 dill pickle, finely chopped

1/2 tsp (2 mL) Dijon mustard

1/4 (1 mL) tsp salt

1/4 tsp (1 mL) black pepper

6 slices bread or 3 buns

Lettuce (optional)

1 Preheat oven to 350°F (180°C). Generously spray a 9- by 5-inch (23 by 12.5 cm) metal loaf pan with nonstick spray; set pan inside a 13- by 9-inch (33 by 23 cm) baking pan and fill with warm water so it comes about 1 inch (2.5 cm) up the sides of the loaf pan.

2 Break eggs into loaf pan and cover pan tightly with foil. Carefully place in oven. Bake 30 to 35 minutes or until eggs are cooked to desired doneness. Remove from oven and cool loaf pan on a wire rack. Use a knife to dice the eggs in the loaf pan.

3 Add mayonnaise, mustard, pickle, salt and pepper; stir to combine. Chill until ready to assemble sandwiches. Spoon filling onto bread or into split buns to make sandwiches. Tuck in lettuce, if using.

TIPS

For something a little extra, add sprouts, bacon bits or chopped olives.

Be sure to use a metal loaf pan, as it heats up quickly and provides consistent, even baking for this recipe. The insulated water bath also helps the eggs to cook evenly.

MAKE AHEAD

The egg salad keeps well in fridge in an airtight container for up to 3 days.

SALMON SANDWICHES

SERVES 2 · (30)

Sometimes you need to change up your salmon salad — and that's what we are here for. Enjoy this twist on a classic.

1 can (27 oz/213 g) sockeye salmon, drained

¼ cup (60 mL) tartar sauce

¼ tsp (1 mL) Old Bay seasoning

¼ tsp (1 mL) grated lemon zest

½ cup (125 mL) baby arugula

2 brioche buns, toasted

4 slices cucumber

2 thin slices red onion (optional)

1 Place salmon in a bowl and, using a fork, mash well, including bones. Stir in tartar sauce, Old Bay seasoning and lemon zest.

2 Divide arugula on bottom half of brioche buns. Divide salmon mixture over arugula and top with cucumber and red onion, if using. Put halves together and serve.

I need salmon like you.

SMASHED WHITE BEAN SAMMIES

SERVES 2 · · ·

Here's a hearty sandwich you can look forward to — it's so good. We love that it's super tasty and filling, with an added crunch from the sunflower seeds.

1 can (19 oz/540 mL) cannellini beans, rinsed and drained

3 tbsp (45 mL) mayonnaise

1 tbsp (15 mL) lemon juice

1 tsp (5 mL) dried dill

1/2 tsp (2 mL) Dijon mustard

1/2 tsp (2 mL) garlic powder

1/4 tsp (1 mL) each salt and black pepper

2 tbsp (30 mL) sunflower seeds

4 slices hearty bread

Lettuce leaves

Thinly sliced red onion

1 small tomato, sliced

1 In a medium bowl, add beans; lightly mash with a fork, leaving some beans whole. Add mayonnaise, lemon juice, dill, mustard, garlic powder, salt and pepper. Taste and season with more salt and pepper if needed.

2 Toast bread and divide the mixture onto 2 slices; then sprinkle with sunflower seeds, top with some lettuce, onion and tomato slices and remaining 2 slices of bread.

TIP

Instead of lettuce leaves, try spinach, sprouts, microgreens or arugula.

MAKE AHEAD

The filling can be made ahead, refrigerated and stored in an airtight container for up to 2 days.

TOFU KATSU SANDWICHES

SERVES 4 ·

Katsu is a Japanese dish of a meat or vegetable covered in breadcrumbs, then fried and served with a sauce. Our tofu version is tasty and flavorful. Sylvia's meat-loving friends gave this sandwich two thumbs up! We've left the crusts on this sandwich but it is often served with the crusts removed. The excess water in the tofu is first pressed to ensure a firmer, chewier piece that doesn't fall apart when cooking.

1 package (10 oz/300 g) package extra firm tofu, pressed and drained

$\frac{1}{2}$ cup (125 mL) panko bread crumbs

2 tbsp (30 mL) cornstarch

$\frac{1}{2}$ tsp (2 mL) onion powder

$\frac{1}{2}$ tsp (2 mL) garlic powder

$\frac{1}{2}$ tsp (2 mL) smoked paprika

$\frac{1}{2}$ tsp (2 mL) salt

1$\frac{1}{2}$ tbsp (22 mL) Dijon mustard

Canola oil for frying

8 slices white bread

Mayonnaise

Teriyaki sauce

Finely shredded cabbage

Pickle slices

1 Slice pressed tofu slab into $\frac{1}{2}$-inch (1 cm) cutlets; pat dry with a paper towel.

2 In a shallow dish, add panko, cornstarch, onion powder, garlic powder, smoked paprika and salt; stir to combine well.

3 Brush cutlets all over with mustard and coat in panko mixture, pressing gently to make sure it adheres.

4 In a large skillet, heat about $\frac{1}{4}$ inch (0.5 cm) of oil over medium heat. Add cutlets and cook until brown and crispy, about 3 minutes per side.

5 To assemble the sandwich, spread a little mayonnaise and teriyaki sauce on 4 slices of bread. Place a tofu cutlet, cabbage, pickle slices and remaining bread slices on top. Serve immediately.

TIPS

To press the tofu, wrap the tofu with a tea towel or paper towels and place on a plate or a baking sheet. Place another a plate or a heavy skillet on top, then weigh it down with a few heavy cans of food. Let sit for 30 minutes. Unwrap the tofu and proceed with recipe.

If extra firm tofu is not available, use firm tofu; however, the texture will be softer.

TURKEY SAUSAGE SANDOS

SERVES 4 · (30) · 🥘

Enjoy this quick meal for lunch or dinner. This is a jazzed-up sloppy joe that is warm and gooey all at the same time. Looking for some added spice? Try a hot Italian turkey sausage instead.

1 tbsp (15 mL) canola oil

1 small onion, chopped

1 small green bell pepper, chopped

2 garlic cloves, minced

1 lb (454 g) mild Italian turkey sausages, casings removed

2 tsp (10 mL) dried oregano leaves

1/4 tsp (1 mL) hot pepper flakes

1 can (19 oz/540 mL) petite-cut stewed tomatoes

2 tbsp (30 mL) tomato paste

2 tsp (10 mL) Worcestershire sauce

1/4 tsp (1 mL) salt

4 Kaiser buns

4 slices provolone cheese

1 cup (250 mL) baby arugula

1 In a large nonstick skillet, heat oil over medium heat and cook onion, pepper and garlic for about 3 minutes or until softened. Add turkey sausage, oregano and hot pepper flakes and cook, breaking up with a wooden spoon for about 5 minutes or until no longer pink.

2 Add tomatoes, tomato paste, Worcestershire sauce and salt. Simmer gently for 15 minutes or until thickened.

3 Open buns and place bottom half on each plate and spoon turkey mixture over top. Top with provolone and arugula. Sandwich with top bun to serve.

TIP
You can substitute your favorite pork or plant-based sausages in this recipe too.

BEEF & VEAL

SLOW COOKER BEEF ENCHILADA MEATBALLS

SERVES 4 · · ·

Easy flavorful meatballs that don't require browning are your
go-to when it comes to simple mealtime prep. We've added
crushed tortillas to keep the meatballs tender and juicy.
Load up the finished dish with optional toppings.

MEATBALLS

1 lb (500 g) lean ground
beef or veal

1/2 cup (125 mL) crushed
jalapeño-flavored tortilla
chips

1 large egg, beaten

1/4 cup (60 mL) finely
chopped green onion

1/4 cup (60 mL) finely
chopped cilantro

1 tsp (5 mL) smoked
paprika

1/2 tsp (2 mL) garlic
powder

1/2 tsp (2 mL) ground cumin

1/2 tsp (2 mL) each salt and
black pepper

SAUCE

2 cups (500 mL) mild salsa

3/4 cup (175 mL) tomato
sauce

1 tsp (5 mL) smoked
paprika

1 tsp (5 mL) dried oregano

1/2 tsp (2 mL) ground cumin

1 cup (250 mL) shredded
Monterey Jack cheese

1 Lightly coat the bottom of a 6-quart slow cooker
with oil or cooking spray.

2 In a large bowl, mix beef, crushed tortilla chips, egg,
green onion, cilantro, paprika, garlic powder, cumin,
salt and pepper until well combined. Using a small
ice-cream scoop or 2-tbsp (30 mL) measure, form
mixture into meatballs. Arrange in a single layer in
bottom of slow cooker.

3 In a bowl, combine sauce ingredients and pour on
top of meatballs. Cover the slow cooker and cook on
High for 2 hours until meatballs are cooked through.
Remove lid and sprinkle cheese over top, then cover
for a few minutes until cheese is melted.

4 Garnish and serve with optional toppings (see tip).

TIPS

Suggested optional toppings include tortilla chips,
lime wedges, avocado or guacamole, cilantro,
green onion, tomatoes, sour cream and fresh
jalapeño peppers.

Refrigerate cooked meatballs for up to 4 days in
an airtight container or freeze for up to 2 months.

FETA MEATBALLS AND BEANS

SERVES 4 · (30) · 🍲

This hearty and easy meal is perfect for those cool fall evenings.
Serve with your favorite garlic bread to sop up all the sauce!

1 lb (500 g) lean ground beef or veal

1/3 cup (75 mL) seasoned dry breadcrumbs

1 large egg

1 tsp (5 mL) onion powder

1 tsp (5 mL) garlic powder

1/2 tsp (2 mL) each salt and black pepper

1 tbsp (15 mL) canola oil

1 can (19 oz/540 mL) cannellini or white kidney beans, drained and rinsed

1 can (19 oz/540 mL) petite-cut tomatoes with garlic and olive oil

1/2 cup (125 mL) crumbled feta cheese

2 tbsp (30 mL) chopped fresh parsley

1 In a large bowl, mix beef, breadcrumbs, egg, onion and garlic powder, salt and pepper until well combined. Use a small ice-cream scoop or 2-tbsp (30 mL) measure to form mixture into meatballs.

2 In a large nonstick skillet, heat oil over medium-high heat. Brown meatballs all over and reduce heat to medium. Add beans and tomatoes and bring to a simmer. Simmer, turning occasionally for about 15 minutes or until meatballs are no longer pink inside and sauce is thickened.

3 Sprinkle feta cheese and parsley all over and let melt slightly before serving.

TIP

You can brown the meatballs and put them in a slow cooker with the tomatoes and beans. Cook on Low for 2 to 3 hours, then stir in feta and parsley to serve.

VEGETABLE BEEF CURRY

SERVES 4 ·

Serve this hearty curry with naan bread or paranthas
so you can wipe up every bit of the sauce on your plate!
It's also delicious served over basmati rice.

1 onion, halved

2 garlic cloves

1 tbsp (15 mL) chopped
fresh ginger

1 small hot chili pepper,
halved and seeded

1 tbsp (15 mL) canola oil

1 tbsp (15 mL) mild curry
powder or paste

8 oz (250 g) lean ground
beef or veal

3 cups (750 mL) water,
divided

1 lb (500 g) sweet
potatoes, peeled and
diced

1 can (19 oz/540 mL)
chickpeas, drained and
rinsed

2 tsp (10 mL) garam masala

$\frac{1}{2}$ tsp (2 mL) salt

$\frac{1}{4}$ cup (60 mL) chopped
fresh cilantro

1 In food processor or mini chop, purée onion, garlic, ginger and chili pepper into a paste.

2 In a large deep skillet or saucepan, heat oil over medium heat and cook onion paste for about 5 minutes or until softened. Stir in curry powder and cook for 1 minute. Add ground beef and cook for 5 minutes to brown.

3 Add 2 cups (500 mL) of the water and stir to make a gravy consistency. Add sweet potatoes; cover and cook, stirring occasionally for about 10 minutes or until sweet potatoes are tender but firm. Add chickpeas, garam masala, salt and remaining water and cook for 10 minutes or until thickened and sweet potatoes are very tender.

4 Sprinkle with cilantro before serving.

TIP
To change it up, use chopped steak or stir-fry strips instead of ground beef.

INSTANT POT BEEF BARBACOA

SERVES 8 ·

If you're looking for a tasty way to serve a crowd, this beef recipe is the solution. This dish is so versatile; enjoy it in a tortilla, taco, burrito or on top of a rice bowl. Whatever you're serving it with, you'll love the flavorful sauce drizzled on top.

1 tbsp (15 mL) canola oil

1 onion, finely chopped

2 lbs (1 kg) boneless beef bottom blade roast or veal, cut into 4 inch/10 cm pieces

1 1/2 tsp (7 mL) salt

1/2 tsp (2 mL) black pepper

5 garlic cloves, minced

1 canned chipotle pepper, finely chopped

1 tbsp (15 mL) adobo sauce (from canned chipotle pepper)

1 tbsp (15 mL) soy sauce

1 tbsp (15 mL) tomato paste

2 tsp (10 mL) chili powder

2 tsp (10 mL) dried oregano

2 tsp (10 mL) ground cumin

1 cup (250 mL) ready-to-use beef broth

2 tbsp (30 mL) cider vinegar

1. In a 6-quart Instant Pot, select Sauté. Add oil and onion; cook 5 minutes, stirring occasionally. Add beef; sprinkle with salt and pepper and sauté 5 minutes, stirring occasionally. Add garlic, chipotle pepper, adobo sauce, soy sauce, tomato paste, chili powder, oregano and cumin; stir to combine. Stir in broth and vinegar.

2. Press Cancel and lock lid; set pressure release valve to Sealing. Press Manual Pressure Cook; set to High for 50 minutes. When cooking finishes let the pressure release naturally for 20 minutes, then release remaining steam by moving the pressure release valve to Venting. Press Cancel; open lid. Transfer beef to a bowl; using two forks, shred beef.

3. While you are shredding the beef, select Sauté on Instant Pot, and cook sauce for 5 minutes to concentrate the sauce. Press Cancel. Ladle some of the sauce on top of beef or serve the sauce on the side.

MAKE AHEAD

Store in an airtight container in the refrigerator for up to 4 days. It can also be frozen for up to 3 months.

SKILLET CANTONESE-STYLE SATAY BEEF

SERVES 5 · ·

There are many versions of satay, including Thai, Indonesian and Malaysian styles. This Cantonese version is is a favorite of Sylvia's family. Serve over hot cooked rice or rice noodles.

BEEF

1 lb (500 g) beef flank steak, sliced into ¼-inch (0.5 cm) slices

1 tbsp (15 mL) each soy sauce, cornstarch and canola oil

¼ tsp (1 mL) baking soda

SAUCE

1½ cups (375 mL) ready-to-use chicken broth

2 tbsp (30 mL) each soy sauce, peanut butter and oyster sauce

1 tbsp (15 mL) cornstarch

2 tsp (10 mL) brown sugar

1 tsp (5 mL) each curry powder, sesame oil and Sriracha

½ tsp (2 mL) each ground coriander, ground cumin and black pepper

STIR-FRY

3 tbsp (45 mL) canola oil, divided

1 medium onion, chopped

2 sweet bell peppers (any color), sliced into ½-inch (1 cm) slices

3 garlic cloves, minced

1 **BEEF:** In a bowl, add beef, soy sauce, cornstarch, oil and baking soda. Stir to combine, making sure beef is evenly coated. Set aside for 20 minutes.

2 **SAUCE:** In a bowl, combine sauce ingredients; set aside.

3 **STIR-FRY:** In a large nonstick skillet, heat 1 tbsp (15 mL) oil over medium-high heat. Add half of the beef, spread out in a single layer and fry for 2 minutes without stirring, then transfer to a plate; beef will still be pink. Repeat with remaining beef.

4 In the same skillet, heat remaining 1 tbsp (15 mL) oil over medium heat, add the onion and stir-fry for 1 minute, stirring often. Add the peppers and garlic; stir-fry for 1 minute, stirring often. Stir sauce mixture to combine, then add to skillet; cook, stirring constantly until sauce thickens, about 30 seconds. Add beef and any accumulated juices back to the skillet, stir-fry until beef is cooked through, about 1 minute. Serve right away.

TIP

For tender beef, slice the flank steak across the grain (against the direction the muscle fibers are running).

VEAL RAVIOLI STEW WITH MUSHROOMS

SERVES 6 TO 8 ·

This whole-meal stew needs a crisp green salad alongside.
And be sure to serve with bread to sop up any juices
remaining in the bowl — you won't regret it.

2 lbs (1 kg) stewing veal or
beef cubes

3 tbsp (45 mL) all-purpose
flour

3/4 tsp (3 mL) each salt and
black pepper, divided

1/2 tsp (2 mL) dried thyme

3 tbsp (45 mL) canola oil,
divided

6 slices bacon, chopped

2 onions, chopped

4 garlic cloves, minced

8 oz (250 g) button
mushrooms, quartered

2 cups (500 mL) veal or
beef broth

1/2 cup (125 mL) heavy or
whipping (35%) cream

8 oz (250 g) fresh ravioli
(cheese or meat)

Chopped parsley
(optional)

1 In a large bowl, toss the veal with flour and 1/2 tsp
(2 mL) each of the salt and pepper and thyme
to coat.

2 In a large shallow Dutch oven, heat 2 tbsp (30 mL) of
the oil over medium-high heat. Brown veal in batches
and return to bowl. Reduce heat to medium. Add
remaining oil and stir in bacon, onions and garlic;
cook, stirring for about 10 minutes or until softened
and brown.

3 Add mushrooms and cook for about 5 minutes or
until starting to brown. Add broth and remaining
salt and pepper; bring to a simmer. Add browned
veal and any juices to the onion mixture. Return to
a simmer, cover and cook, stirring occasionally, for
about 1 1/2 hours or until veal is tender.

4 Stir in cream, add ravioli and cook, uncovered,
stirring occasionally for about 8 minutes or until
ravioli are tender. Serve in shallow bowls garnished
with parsley, if desired.

VIETNAMESE-STYLE BEEF STEW

SERVES 8

Bo Kho is a flavorful favorite Vietnamese dish in Sylvia's home. Although it is called a stew, it's traditionally more brothy and served with a baguette, flat rice noodles or rice. Be sure to customize your bowl with plenty of fresh garnishes.

1 tbsp (15 mL) canola oil

1 onion, thinly sliced

1 piece (2 inches/5 cm) fresh ginger, peeled, cut in half

¼ cup (60 mL) tomato paste

5 garlic cloves, minced

1 tbsp (15 mL) paprika

2 tsp (10 mL) Chinese five-spice powder

1 tsp (5 mL) black pepper

½ tsp (2 mL) ground cinnamon

3 stalks lemongrass, cut into 5-inch/12.5 cm lengths, pounded

3 cups (750 mL) ready-to-use chicken broth

2 cups (500 mL) water

¼ cup (60 mL) fish sauce

1 tbsp (15 mL) brown sugar

2 lbs (1 kg) boneless beef blade or veal roast, cut into 1-inch (2.5 cm) pieces

8 medium carrots, cut into 1½-inch (4 cm) pieces

Salt

1. In a 6-quart Instant Pot, select Sauté. Heat oil for 10 seconds, then add onion and ginger and cook for 2 minutes, stirring occasionally. Add tomato paste, garlic, paprika, five-spice powder, pepper and cinnamon; cook for 30 seconds, stirring often. Add lemongrass, broth, water, fish sauce and brown sugar, scraping up any browned bits. Add beef and carrots.

2. Press Cancel and lock lid; set pressure release valve to Sealing. Press Manual Pressure Cook; set to High for 25 minutes. When cooking finishes, let the pressure release naturally for 20 minutes, then release the remaining steam by moving the pressure release valve to Venting. Press Cancel; open lid. Discard ginger and lemongrass. Season with salt to taste. Serve with garnishes suggested in tip below.

TIP
Add garnishes and enjoy the fresh boost of flavor they provide. Suggested garnishes include lime wedges, cilantro, mint, Thai basil, jalapeno pepper slices, Sriracha and raw onion slices.

MAKE AHEAD
Refrigerate and store the stew in an airtight container for up to 3 days.

SHEET-PAN BEEF AND MUSHROOM FAJITAS

SERVES 4 ·  ·

Fajitas are a winner at our dinner table. It's always fun to enjoy fajitas when they're served along with all the fresh toppings set on the table so family and guests can build their own favorite flavor pairings.

3 tbsp (45 mL) canola oil

2 tsp (10 mL) ground cumin

2 tsp (10 mL) ground coriander

2 tsp (10 mL) chili powder

1 tsp (5 ml) each salt and black pepper

1 lb (500 g) beef stir-fry strips

1 portobello mushroom, thinly sliced (about 8 oz/250 g)

1 small onion, thinly sliced

2 bell peppers (any color), cut into $\frac{1}{2}$-inch (1 cm) slices

12 to 16 small soft corn or flour tortillas, warmed

TOPPINGS (OPTIONAL)

Salsa

Avocado

Sour cream

Cilantro

Hot sauce

Lime wedges

1 Place one oven rack in the middle and another about 5 inches (12.5 cm) from the top. Preheat oven to 425°F (220°C). Set aside a rimmed baking sheet.

2 In a bowl, combine oil, cumin, coriander, chili powder, salt and pepper. Add beef, mushroom, onion and peppers; gently toss to combine. Spread mixture on prepared pan in a single layer; bake on middle rack 15 minutes.

3 Turn oven to broil and move baking sheet to top rack. Broil until meat and vegetables are lightly charred, about 3 to 5 minutes. Serve with tortillas and your favorite toppings.

TIPS

Line baking sheet with foil for easier cleanup.

To warm the tortillas stack, wrap them in foil and place in the oven for 5 minutes during the last few minutes of baking. Or wrap a stack of tortillas in parchment paper and microwave them on high for about 30 to 40 seconds until warmed through. Keep wrapped until ready to serve.

For a crunchy version, substitute hard tortillas for the soft tortillas.

MAKE AHEAD

Slice vegetables up to 2 days ahead; cover and refrigerate until ready to cook.

CAST-IRON STEAK WITH MUSHROOM BUTTER SAUCE

SERVES 4 ·

Sometimes you just need to celebrate the deliciousness of a simple steak. This creamy rich sauce is exactly the right finishing touch!

MUSHROOM BUTTER SAUCE

1/3 cup (75 mL) unsalted butter, divided

2 tbsp (30 mL) minced shallot

1 cup (250 mL) chopped mushrooms

3/4 cup (175 mL) heavy or whipping (35%) cream

1 tbsp (15 mL) tomato paste

2 tbsp (30 mL) chopped fresh parsley

Pinch each salt and black pepper

STEAKS

4 beef tenderloin steaks, ribeye or top sirloin medallions (about 1 lb/500 g total)

1 tbsp (15 mL) barbecue spice rub

1 tbsp (15 mL) canola oil

1 MUSHROOM BUTTER SAUCE: In a cast-iron skillet, melt 2 tbsp (30 mL) of the butter over medium heat. Add shallot and cook for 2 minutes or until softened. Add mushrooms and cook for about 5 minutes or until starting to brown.

2 Whisk together cream and tomato paste; add to skillet. Reduce heat and simmer for about 3 minutes or until reduced by half. Whisk in remaining butter, 1 tbsp (15 mL) at a time, until smooth, creamy and thickened enough to coat a spoon. Stir in parsley, salt and pepper; scrape into a bowl and cover to keep warm.

3 STEAKS: Wipe out cast-iron skillet well and heat over medium-high heat until almost smoking. Meanwhile, rub steaks with spice rub. Add oil to skillet and swirl around. Sear steaks about 5 minutes per side for medium-rare or until desired doneness. Remove steaks from pan and let stand for 3 minutes.

4 Place steaks on plates and spoon Mushroom Butter Sauce over top to serve.

CHICKEN & TURKEY

CRISPY JAPANESE-STYLE CHICKEN BITES

SERVES 4 · 5

These tasty baked bites are inspired by Menchi Katsu,
a popular Japanese deep-fried ground meat cutlet. Enjoy these
bites in a sandwich or serve with rice and a vegetable side dish.
Toasting the crumbs is the secret to the crunch and
color of these crispy meatballs.

1 cup (250 mL) panko
 bread crumbs

1 lb (500 g) ground chicken
 or turkey

1 large egg, lightly beaten

1 tsp (5 mL) Worcestershire
 sauce

1/2 tsp (2 mL) onion powder

1/2 tsp (2 mL) salt

1/4 tsp (1 mL) black pepper

Canola oil for drizzling

Ketchup

1 Preheat oven to 400°F (200°C). Spread the panko
   in an even layer on a rimmed baking sheet and
   bake 5 minutes or until light golden brown, stirring
   halfway through baking. Watch carefully, as panko
   can easily burn. Remove from oven and transfer
   to a shallow dish to cool.

2 When the baking sheet has cooled, spray lightly with
   nonstick cooking spray; set aside.

3 In a bowl, add chicken, egg, Worcestershire,
   onion powder, salt, pepper and 3 tbsp (45 mL) of
   toasted panko; mix until combined. Using a small ice
   cream scoop or a 2-tbsp (30 mL) measure, shape
   mixture into balls, then press gently into patties
   about 2 inches (5 cm) wide and 1/2 inch (1 cm) thick.
   Completely coat each bite in remaining panko,
   pressing gently to help the panko to stick.

4 Place on prepared baking sheet and drizzle
   a little oil over each bite. Bake for 20 minutes
   or until cooked through. Serve with additional
   Worcestershire sauce or ketchup for dipping.
   Makes about 20 bites.

TIP
Line the baking sheet with foil for easier cleanup.

MAKE AHEAD
You can toast the panko 2 days ahead of time;
store in an airtight container

QUICK CHICKEN COCONUT CURRY

SERVES 4 TO 5 ·  ·

A supermarket rotisserie chicken is a welcome shortcut
to get this fragrant meal on the table in very little time.
Serve with rice and your favorite steamed vegetables.

1 tbsp (15 mL) canola oil

1 small onion, chopped

1 tbsp (15 mL) Thai red
curry paste

2 garlic cloves, minced

1 can (14 oz/540 mL)
coconut milk

1 cup (250 mL) ready-to-
use chicken broth

2 tbsp (30 mL) light brown
sugar

1 tbsp (15 mL) fish sauce

1 tbsp (15 mL) soy sauce

4 cups (1 L) chopped
cooked chicken

1/4 cup (60 mL) chopped
cilantro leaves and stems

2 stalks green onion, thinly
sliced

2 tbsp (30 mL) lime juice

1 In a large pot, heat oil over medium-high heat; add
onion and cook 5 minutes, stirring occasionally. Stir
in curry paste and garlic, cook 30 seconds, then
add coconut milk, broth, brown sugar, fish sauce
and soy sauce; stir to combine. Bring to a boil, then
reduce heat to medium. Simmer for 5 to 10 minutes
to thicken the sauce slightly.

2 Add chicken, cover and cook 5 minutes or until
chicken is heated through. Remove from heat; stir in
cilantro, green onion and lime juice. Serve with hot
cooked rice or rice noodles.

MAKE AHEAD

Have the vegetables and chicken chopped and
refrigerated the night before so you've got a head
start on cooking this speedy meal.

Cook rice the night before and refrigerate. Simply
reheat when you're ready to eat.

SHEET-PAN CHICKEN SHAWARMA

SERVES 6 ·

Simplicity in a delicious oven meal — this is one that we like to prepare on repeat. This Middle Eastern-inspired recipe uses yogurt and warm spices to marinate the chicken, which helps make the chicken tender and flavorful. Make sure there are plenty of toppings such as tomato, cucumber, lettuce, onion and feta cheese.

½ cup (125 mL) plain yogurt

5 garlic cloves, minced

1 tbsp (15 mL) smoked paprika

1½ tsp (7 mL) salt

1 tsp (5 mL) ground coriander

1 tsp (5 mL) ground cumin

1 tsp (5 mL) ground turmeric

1 tsp (5 mL) ground cinnamon

1 tsp (5 mL) ground cardamom

1½ lbs (750 g) boneless, skinless chicken thighs, sliced into 1-inch (2.5 cm) strips

2 tbsp (30 mL) canola oil (divided)

1 red bell pepper, sliced

1 yellow bell pepper, sliced

1 onion, thinly sliced

Hummus

6 pita bread

1 Place one oven rack in the middle position and another about 5 inches (12.5 cm) below the broiler. Preheat oven to 425°F (220° C); set aside a large rimmed baking sheet.

2 In a bowl, combine yogurt, garlic, paprika, salt, coriander, cumin, turmeric, cinnamon and cardamom. Add chicken and stir until evenly coated. Marinate 15 minutes.

3 Drizzle baking sheet with 1 tbsp (15 mL) of the oil, then arrange chicken, peppers and onion in an even layer, then drizzle with remaining oil. Bake on the middle rack for 12 minutes or until chicken is cooked through; stir ingredients halfway through cooking time. Turn on broiler, move baking sheet to top rack and broil 3 minutes or until meat and vegetables are slightly charred.

4 Spread a generous portion of hummus on each pita bread, then add chicken and roasted vegetables along with plenty of suggested toppings.

TIPS

Line the baking sheet with foil for easier cleanup.

Try other flatbread options such as balady, naan, tortilla or lavash.

CHICKEN AND CORN PARMESAN OVEN RISOTTO

SERVES 4 TO 6 ·

No standing at the stove is required to finish this risotto! Creamy and filling, this all-in-one meal is a family favorite.

1/3 cup (75 mL) unsalted butter, divided

2 small boneless skinless chicken breasts (about 8 oz/250 g), chopped

1 tsp (5 mL) dried thyme

1/4 tsp (1 mL) each salt and black pepper

1 onion, finely chopped

2 cups (500 mL) arborio rice

2 garlic cloves, minced

1/3 cup (75 mL) dry white wine

2 1/4 cups (560 mL) ready-to-use chicken or vegetable broth

1 cup (250 mL) half-and-half (10%) cream

3/4 cup (175 mL) grated Parmesan cheese

3/4 cup (175 mL) fresh or thawed corn kernels

Chopped fresh basil or parsley

1 Preheat oven to 350°F (180°C).

2 In a shallow Dutch oven, melt 2 tbsp (30 mL) of the butter over medium heat. In a bowl, toss chicken with thyme, salt and pepper. Brown chicken and remove to a plate. Add onion to pot and cook for 2 minutes, stirring occasionally.

3 Add rice and garlic; cook, stirring for 30 seconds. Add wine and scrape up any brown bits from the bottom of the pot. Stir in chicken and any accumulated juices, broth and cream. Cover and bake for 30 minutes or until rice is tender and liquid is almost all absorbed.

4 Stir in Parmesan, corn and remaining butter until creamy. Sprinkle with basil to serve and more Parmesan over top if desired.

CHICKEN AND GRAPE TOMATO PASTA

SERVES 4 TO 6

Having cooked pasta in the fridge is what makes this dinner fast. Sweet grape tomatoes and chicken create a delicious sauce with a hit of salty pancetta and anchovies that makes this dish a unique and memorable one for any table.

1 pkg (5 oz/150 g) diced pancetta

3 small boneless, skinless chicken breasts (12 oz/375 g), chopped

Pinch each salt and black pepper

2 cups (500 mL) grape tomatoes, halved

1 cup (250 mL) ready-to-use chicken broth

2 tbsp (30 mL) extra virgin olive oil

4 garlic cloves, minced

4 anchovy fillets, finely chopped

4 cups (1 L) cooked short pasta (such as rotini, penne or fusilli)

2 tbsp (30 mL) chopped fresh parsley

Fresh Parmesan cheese (optional)

1 In a large shallow saucepan, sauté pancetta, stirring often over medium heat for about 10 minutes or until fat is rendered and pancetta is crisp. Remove pancetta to plate and remove all but 1 tbsp (15 mL) of the rendered fat.

2 Meanwhile, sprinkle chicken with salt and pepper and add to saucepan with tomatoes. Pour in broth and bring to a boil. Cover and simmer for about 5 minutes or until chicken is no longer pink inside. Uncover and add oil, garlic and anchovies. Cook for 2 minutes.

3 Stir in pasta and cook for about 5 minutes or until heated through. Stir in parsley and sprinkle with pancetta to serve. Sprinkle with Parmesan, if using.

TIP

To cook pasta, bring a pot of salted water to boil. Cook pasta for about 8 minutes or until al dente. Drain and rinse with cold water. Drain again and drizzle with a little canola oil. You can store the pasta in a sealable bag or airtight container in the fridge or up to 5 days. It's great to use in one pot meals like this one!

SKILLET-ROASTED GARLIC DIJON CHICKEN

SERVES 4 · ·  ·

Cooking the garlic helps soften the flavor and mashing it helps thicken the sauce. This is truly an easy meal that almost creates its own gravy, which is great for the chicken and, if you serve it with mashed potatoes, there is enough to serve over top.

1 head garlic

2 tbsp (30 mL) extra virgin olive oil

8 small bone-in chicken thighs (about 1½ lbs/750 g)

½ tsp (2 mL) each salt and black pepper

1½ cups (375 mL) ready-to-use chicken broth

4 tsp (20 mL) Dijon mustard

2 tbsp (30 mL) chopped fresh parsley

1 Separate and peel cloves of garlic to get about 10 cloves.

2 In a large nonstick skillet, heat oil over medium heat. Add garlic; cover and cook, shaking pan gently for 5 minutes or until starting to become golden and softened. Pour garlic and oil into a small bowl.

3 Sprinkle chicken all over with salt and pepper. Return skillet to medium-high heat and brown chicken on both sides. Reduce heat to medium.

4 Meanwhile, remove garlic cloves from oil and reserve oil for another use. Mash garlic cloves with a fork and stir together with chicken broth and mustard. Pour into skillet with chicken and stir to combine. Bring to a simmer and cook, uncovered, turning chicken occasionally for about 15 minutes or until chicken is no longer pink. Sprinkle with parsley to serve.

TIP

Refrigerate garlic oil for up to 3 days and use in other recipes to add a hint of garlic flavor.

TURKEY SALTIMBOCCA WITH MUSHROOMS

SERVES 4 ·

Saltimbocca means "jump in mouth," and your mouth will surely jump with the lively flavors of fresh lemon and basil.

4 turkey scallopine (about 12 oz/375 g total)

2 tbsp (30 mL) chopped fresh parsley

2 tsp (10 mL) grated lemon zest

1/2 tsp (2 mL) black pepper

8 large fresh basil leaves

8 slices prosciutto or serrano ham

2 tbsp (30 mL) canola oil, divided

8 oz (250 g) button mushrooms, sliced

2 small garlic cloves, minced

1/4 tsp (1 mL) salt

1/2 cup (125 mL) ready-to-use vegetable or chicken broth

1 In a large bowl, toss scallopine with parsley, lemon zest and pepper. Lay scallopine on work surface and top each with basil leaves to cover. Wrap each with prosciutto, using two slices to cover each; set aside.

2 In a large nonstick skillet, heat half of the oil over medium-high heat. Cook mushrooms, garlic and salt for about 8 minutes or until golden and liquid has evaporated. Scrape into a bowl.

3 Return skillet to medium heat and add remaining oil. Add turkey and cook, turning once for about 8 minutes or until prosciutto is crisp and turkey is no longer pink inside. Return mushrooms to skillet with broth and bring to a simmer.

TIP

Substitute chicken scallopine or cutlets for the turkey. Or make your own scallopine by slicing a boneless skinless turkey breast into thin slices and pounding each cutlet into about 1/4-inch (5 mm) thick pieces.

TROPICAL TURKEY SKILLET

SERVES 4 ·

Tropical fruit flavors of coconut, mango and pineapple along with warm spices pair perfectly in this quick dinner best served with your favorite rice dish to sop up all the juices.

2 tbsp (30 mL) canola oil

1 onion, diced

1 celery stalk, diced

2 garlic cloves, minced

1 tbsp (15 mL) minced fresh ginger

1 boneless skinless turkey breast (about 1 lb/500 g), chopped

2 tsp (10 mL) curry powder

1/2 tsp (2 mL) salt

1/2 cup (125 mL) coconut milk

1/2 cup (125 mL) pineapple or orange juice

1 tbsp (15 mL) cornstarch

1 cup (250 mL) chopped mango

1/2 cup (125 mL) diced pineapple

1 small red hot chili pepper, seeded and sliced (optional)

1/2 tsp (2 mL) grated lime zest

1 tbsp (15 mL) lime juice

1/2 cup (125 mL) chopped roasted cashews (optional)

1 In a large nonstick skillet, heat oil over medium heat and cook onion, celery, garlic and ginger for about 3 minutes or until softened. Increase heat to medium high and add turkey, curry powder and salt. Sauté until turkey is browned.

2 In a small bowl, whisk together coconut milk, pineapple juice and cornstarch. Pour into skillet and stir to coat turkey. Bring to a simmer and add mango, pineapple, chili pepper if using, lime zest and juice. Cook, stirring occasionally for about 5 minutes or until turkey is no longer pink inside. Sprinkle with cashews, if using, to serve.

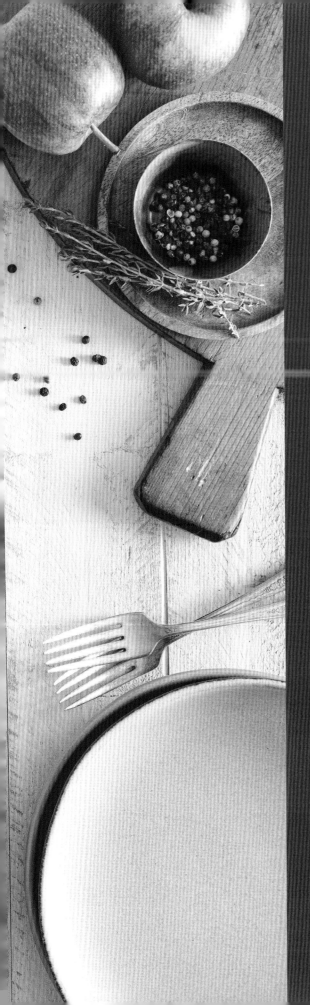

PORK & LAMB

SMOKED HAM AND CHEESE SCONES

MAKES 8 BISCUITS · ·

The smokiness of the ham and buttery creamy flavor of Havarti cheese are perfectly paired in every bite. Our method of cutting and stacking the dough creates multiple layers of flaky goodness.

2 cups (500 mL) all-purpose flour

1 tbsp (15 mL) baking powder

1 tsp (5 mL) granulated sugar

1 tsp (5 mL) salt

1 tsp (5 mL) black pepper

1/2 tsp (2 mL) garlic powder

1/2 cup (125 mL) butter, cold and cubed

1 1/2 cups (375 mL) shredded Havarti cheese

1 1/2 cups (375 mL) cubed cooked smoked ham (1/4-inch/0.5 cm pieces)

1/4 cup (60 mL) finely chopped green onion

3/4 cup (175 mL) half-and-half (10%) cream

1 large egg beaten with 1 tbsp (15 mL) water

1/4 cup (60 mL) grated Parmesan cheese

1 Preheat oven to 425°F (220°C); set aside a lightly greased or parchment paper lined baking sheet.

2 In a large bowl, combine flour, baking powder, sugar, salt, pepper and garlic powder. Add butter; using a pastry blender or two forks, cut into flour until mixture is crumbly. Add cheese, ham and green onions; toss until ingredients are evenly distributed in mixture. Drizzle cream overtop and gently combine to make a ragged dough.

3 On a lightly floured surface, pat dough into a 9-inch (23 cm) square; cut into 4 squares, stack them on top of each other. Repeat process. Pat into a 9 inch (23 cm) square, then divide dough into 8 pieces. Transfer to prepared baking sheet; brush tops with egg wash and evenly sprinkle Parmesan cheese on top. Bake 25 to 30 minutes, until golden. Transfer to a rack to cool.

TIPS

Enjoy these biscuits as sandwiches. Slice biscuits in half horizontally and fill with a fried egg and arugula.

Chives can be substituted for the green onions.

Monterey Jack cheese can substitute for the Havarti.

MAKE AHEAD

You can chill the dough overnight once it's at the last rolled-out stage. Wrap well and store in the refrigerator.

INSTANT POT PORK TENDERLOIN

SERVES 4 ·

Pork is best enjoyed when it's juicy, tender and has a hint of pink. This simple, delicious pork tenderloin is perfect for entertaining or any night of the week.

1 tbsp (15 mL) canola oil, plus a little for rubbing on tenderloin

1 (1 lb/500 g) pork tenderloin, silver skin removed

2 tsp (10 mL) dried Italian seasoning

1 tsp (5 mL) black pepper

1/2 cup (125 mL) ready-to-use chicken broth

2 tbsp (30 mL) Dijon mustard

1 tbsp (15 mL) grainy mustard

1 tsp (5 mL) soy sauce

1/2 cup (125 mL) heavy or whipping (35%) cream

1 tsp (5 mL) cornstarch

1 In a 6-quart Instant Pot, select Sauté, add oil. Pat tenderloin dry with paper towel. Rub a little oil on the tenderloin, then sprinkle meat with Italian seasoning and pepper. Add pork to pot and sear on all sides, about 5 minutes. Remove to a plate.

2 Add the chicken broth to the pot and scrape up browned bits in the bottom of pot. Stir in mustards and soy sauce, then return tenderloin to pot. Press Cancel and lock lid; set pressure release valve to Sealing. Press Manual Pressure Cook; set to High for 4 minutes. When cooking finishes; quick-release the steam by moving the pressure valve to Venting. Press Cancel, then carefully open the lid.

3 Transfer pork to a serving plate. An instant-read thermometer inserted in the thickest part of the tenderloin should register 145°F (63°C). Let rest 5 minutes. If meat requires more cook time, return to pot for a moment to finish cooking in the sauce to desired doneness.

4 Select Sauté and bring sauce to a boil for 2 minutes. Whisk together the cream and cornstarch, then whisk mixture into sauce; cook for 1 minute. Press Cancel. Slice the pork, spoon sauce over top and serve.

TIP

To trim the tenderloin, start at one end of the meat and slip a knife under the silver skin (the white tough connective tissue). Carefully guide the knife along the meat while pulling the silver skin away.

SHEET-PAN SAUSAGE, APPLE AND ONION BAKE

SERVES 4 ·

This is simple and satisfying comfort food that will make your kitchen smell welcoming. Serve with a side salad and some hearty bread.

1 large red onion, cut into 1/2-inch (1 cm) strips

2 apples, cut into 1-inch (2.5 cm) slices

2 garlic cloves, peeled and crushed

1 tbsp (15 mL) canola oil

1 tsp (5 mL) dried rosemary

1 tsp (5 mL) dried thyme

1/2 tsp (2 mL) salt

1/4 tsp (1 mL) black pepper

1 1/2 lbs (750 g) mild Italian sausages, about 4 links

Grainy mustard

1 Preheat oven to 425°F (220°C). Line a large rimmed baking sheet with foil. Place onion, apples and garlic on sheet and drizzle with oil. Sprinkle with rosemary, thyme, salt and pepper; toss to evenly coat. Place sausages on the baking pan, making sure they have direct contact with the pan for even cooking. Arrange ingredients in a single layer. Use a small sharp knife to pierce sausages a few times to prevent them from bursting open.

2 Bake 20 minutes, flip the sausages over and bake another 15 minutes or until sausages are cooked through and the onions and apples are tender. Serve with grainy mustard on the side.

TIPS

If the sausages are very thick in diameter, cut in half to ensure they are fully cooked in 20 minutes. An inserted thermometer should register 160°F (71°C).

Apple varieties suitable for baking are Honeycrisp, Braeburn, Pink Lady, Gala and Granny Smith.

RUSTIC SAUSAGE, BEAN AND VEGETABLE STEW

SERVES 8 ·

A hearty stew is perfect for chilly days. Sylvia's family loves this soup so she often makes an extra batch to freeze and have on hand. Serve this with a side of crusty bread or our delicious Zucchini Skillet Cornbread (see page 193).

2 tbsp (30 mL) canola oil

1 large onion, chopped

10 oz (300 g) spicy Italian sausage, casings removed

3 celery stalks, chopped

2 carrots, chopped

6 cups (1.5 L) chopped kale leaves

1 red bell pepper, chopped

2 tsp (10 mL) dried Italian seasoning

4 garlic cloves, minced

4 cups (1 L) ready-to-use chicken or vegetable broth

1 can (28 oz/796 mL) diced tomatoes

2 cans (19 oz/540 mL) navy beans, rinsed and drained

1 cup (250 mL) chopped fresh parsley

Salt and black pepper

Grated Parmesan cheese

1 In a large pot, heat oil over medium-high heat. Add onion and sauté for 5 minutes, stirring occasionally. Add sausage and break it up into bite-size pieces with a wooden spoon; cook 5 minutes. Add celery, carrots, kale, red pepper, Italian seasoning and garlic and cook for 5 minutes, stirring occasionally. Add broth, tomatoes, beans and parsley; bring to boil. Cover and reduce heat to medium; let simmer 30 minutes or until vegetables are tender. Season with salt and pepper to taste.

2 Ladle into bowls and sprinkle with Parmesan on top.

TIP
Cannellini (white kidney beans) or great Northern beans can be substituted for the navy beans.

MAKE AHEAD
This soup freezes well for up to 2 months. Freeze in smaller portions for faster defrosting and for the days when you're not feeding a crowd

PORK CHOP AND VEGGIE SHEET-PAN DINNER

SERVES 4 ·

Sheet-pan dinners are a meal maker's dream and an easy way to combine protein and veggies. Use your favorite barbecue sauce for the pork chops and have extra to serve alongside.

1 lb (500 g) mini potatoes, halved

1 bag (12 oz/375 g) baby carrots

1 small red onion, cut into wedges

3 garlic cloves, minced

2 tbsp (30 mL) canola oil

2 tsp (10 mL) chopped fresh rosemary

$\frac{1}{2}$ tsp (2 mL) each salt and black pepper, divided

4 pork loin boneless center-cut chops (about 1 lb/500 g total)

$\frac{1}{4}$ cup (60 mL) barbecue sauce

1 tbsp (15 mL) chopped fresh parsley

1 Preheat oven to 425°F (220°C). Line a rimmed baking sheet with parchment paper.

2 Spread potatoes, carrots, onion and garlic on prepared baking sheet. Drizzle with oil and sprinkle with rosemary and half each of the salt and pepper. Toss gently to coat. Roast for 10 minutes.

3 Meanwhile, toss pork chops with remaining salt and pepper. Add barbecue sauce and parsley; toss to coat well. Add pork chops to baking sheet and return to oven for 15 minutes or until pork is no longer pink inside and thermometer inserted in pork reaches 155°F (68°C).

TIPS

Look for pork chops about $\frac{3}{4}$ inch (2 cm) thick for a great juicy chop.

Substitute a red bell pepper for the onion for a change in flavor.

**What do you call a pig that knows karate?
A pork chop.**

CIDER-GLAZED BACON-WRAPPED PORK

SERVES 4 ·

You can use your favorite local cider for this recipe — with or without alcohol, it's a winner! Be sure to have mashed potatoes on the plate to soak up the goodness and enjoy every bite.

1 pork tenderloin (about 1 lb/500 g)

¼ tsp (1 mL) black pepper

4 slices bacon

1 tbsp (15 mL) canola oil

1 small red onion, sliced

1 tsp (5 mL) dried sage

1 tsp (5 mL) dried thyme

¼ tsp (1 mL) salt

1 tbsp (15 mL) all-purpose flour

1 cup (250 mL) apple cider

2 tbsp (30 mL) butter

1 Cut tenderloin into 8 even chunks and sprinkle with pepper. Cut bacon strips in half. Wrap each tenderloin piece with half a slice of bacon.

2 In a large skillet, heat oil over medium-high. Brown bacon-wrapped pork pieces well all over. Remove to a plate.

3 Reduce heat to medium and add onion, sage, thyme and salt. Cook, stirring for about 8 minutes or until starting to brown and soften. Stir in flour to coat well. Whisk in cider and bring to a simmer. Return pork to skillet and reduce heat to low and cook for about 8 minutes, turning pork occasionally until hint of pink remains in pork. Add butter and stir until melted.

TIP

You can use alcoholic or non-alcoholic cider for this recipe. Unsweetened is best!

HOT HOISIN RIBS

SERVES 2 TO 3 ·

Ribs in a skillet? You betcha! These are finger-licking good, with a kick of heat, so have cleanup towels ready.

1 rack pork back ribs (about 1½ lbs/750 g)

½ cup (125 mL) ready-to-use vegetable or chicken broth

¼ cup (60 mL) hoisin sauce

2 tbsp (30 mL) soy sauce

2 tbsp (30 mL) rice vinegar

1 tbsp (15 mL) minced fresh ginger

2 garlic cloves, minced

1 tbsp (15 mL) liquid honey

1 tbsp (15 mL) sesame oil

1 tbsp (15 mL) Sriracha

2 green onions, thinly sliced

1   Remove membrane from back bones of ribs and discard. Cut in between bones of ribs to separate.

2   In a bowl, whisk together broth, hoisin sauce, soy sauce, rice vinegar, ginger and garlic; set aside.

3   In a large nonstick skillet, heat oil over medium-high heat and brown ribs all over. Reduce heat to medium and pour in sauce. Toss the ribs in the sauce and partially cover with a lid. Reduce heat to keep a gentle simmer and cook, turning occasionally for about 30 minutes or until ribs are tender.

4   Uncover, stir in honey, sesame oil and Sriracha and cook for about 2 minutes or until sauce is thickened and ribs are well coated. Sprinkle with green onions to serve.

If I tell you I'm thinking about you, don't get too excited, because I'm also thinking about ribs.

SPICY SZECHUAN PORK ROAST

SERVES 10 TO 12 · ·

The garlic and onion crust provides a flavorful bite to the pork. This special roast is delicious served hot and, if there's any left over, you can enjoy it cold the next day in a salad or sandwich.

1/4 cup (60 mL) dry sherry

3 tbsp (45 mL) soy sauce

2 tbsp (30 mL) sesame oil

4 garlic cloves, minced

2 green onions, minced

1 tsp (5 mL) hot pepper flakes

1/2 tsp (2 mL) black peppercorns, crushed

1 boneless pork loin center-cut roast, about 3 lbs/1.5 kg

1 In a large sealable bag, combine sherry, soy sauce, sesame oil, garlic, green onions, hot pepper flakes and peppercorns. Add roast and turn to coat well. Seal bag and refrigerate to marinate for at least 8 hours or up to 24 hours.

2 Preheat oven to 375°F (190°C). Line a roasting pan with foil and place rack on top of foil.

3 Place roast fat side up in prepared pan and reserve marinade. Roast for about 1 hour and 45 minutes or until temperature reaches 155°F (68°C), brushing liberally with reserved marinade for the first hour of cooking. Tent with foil and let stand 5 minutes before slicing thinly to serve.

*"Hey buddy, are you a pork roast?
'Cause you are really well done."*

LAMB SHOULDER CHOPS WITH OLIVES

SERVES 4 · (30) · 🍲

Lamb this easy sounds improbable but it isn't. You're going to want to serve this up for family and friends often. A simple little rice pilaf and veggies alongside make it a winning meal.

4 lamb shoulder chops (about 1½ lbs/750 g total)

¼ tsp (1 mL) each salt and black pepper

2 tbsp (30 mL) canola oil

2 sprigs fresh rosemary

2 garlic cloves

½ cup (125 mL) dry white wine

½ cup (125 mL) pitted cracked green or small green olives

Half a lemon

2 tbsp (30 mL) butter

2 tbsp (30 mL) chopped fresh parsley

1 Sprinkle lamb chops with salt and pepper.

2 In a large nonstick skillet, heat oil, rosemary and garlic over medium-low heat. Cook, turning rosemary often, for about 5 minutes or until fragrant. Increase heat to medium-high heat, add lamb chops and brown both sides well. Remove to a plate.

3 Reduce heat to medium and add wine; simmer for 1 minute. Add olives, squeeze lemon juice from lemon half into skillet with butter and parsley. Return lamb chops to skillet and cook, turning occasionally, for about 8 minutes or until chops reach an internal temperature of 145°F (63°C) for medium-rare or until desired doneness.

FISH & SEAFOOD

SHRIMP BOIL

SERVES 6 · 🚫 · 🍲

A seafood boil is fun way to eat. This meal is traditionally
served on a large platter for everyone to enjoy family style,
but you can also serve in individual bowls. Be sure to have
plenty of napkins for the delicious but messy meal.
Serve with a fresh green salad or coleslaw on the side.

8 cups (2 L) water

1 lemon, quartered

1 red onion, cut into
6 wedges

8 garlic cloves

1/4 cup (60 mL) Old Bay
seasoning

1 1/2 lbs (750 g) baby yellow
or red potatoes, halved

1 tbsp (15 mL) salt

3 ears corn, each cut into
4 pieces

1 lb (500 g) smoked
sausage, cut into 1-inch
(2.5 cm) pieces

1 1/2 lbs (750 g) large raw
shrimp, unpeeled and
deveined

Seasoned Butter (see
recipe)

1 In a large pot, add water, lemons, onion, garlic and
Old Bay seasoning. Cover and bring to a boil over
medium-high heat. Add potatoes, return to boil, then
reduce heat to medium; cover and cook for 10 to
12 minutes or until almost cooked through.

2 Add corn and sausage, cover and cook another
5 to 6 minutes, until sausage is cooked through.
Add shrimp, cook about 2 minutes, until just pink
and opaque.

3 Drain shrimp boil and arrange on a platter or
a rimmed baking sheet. Drizzle a little of the
Seasoned Butter (see below) over top, saving
the rest for dipping.

TIPS

The shrimp shells add flavor to this dish; however,
you can also use peeled shrimp.

Serve with sourdough bread or our delicious
Zucchini Skillet Cornbread (see page 193).

SEASONED BUTTER

In a small serving bowl, combine 1/2 cup (125 mL)
melted butter, 3 tbsp (45 mL) chopped fresh
parsley, 1 tbsp (15 mL) lemon juice, 2 tsp (10 mL)
Worcestershire sauce, 1 tsp (5 mL) Old Bay
seasoning, 1 garlic clove, minced, and 1/4 tsp (1 mL)
black pepper. Keep warm.

BAKED COD WITH FENNEL AND OLIVES

SERVES 4 ·

Here's an easy dinner of tender, juicy baked fish.
First you bake a base of fennel and onions to develop a delicious
flavor and caramelize the edges. Then you top this with the fish
and olives for an additional quick bake. Before you know it,
you'll be ready to eat.

1 fennel bulb

1 red onion, thinly sliced

1 tsp (5 mL) dried Italian seasoning

1/4 tsp (1 mL) hot pepper flakes

2 garlic cloves, sliced in half

2 tbsp (30 mL) olive oil, divided

4 skinless cod fillets (about 6 oz/175 g each)

1/4 tsp (1 mL) each salt and black pepper

3/4 cup (175 mL) pitted black or green olives, sliced in half

2 tbsp (30 mL) chopped fresh parsley

1 Preheat oven to 425°F (220°C).

2 Remove the fennel fronds and stalks, then slice the bulb thinly. Set aside fronds for garnishing, if available.

3 On a rimmed baking sheet, place fennel, onion, Italian seasoning, hot pepper flakes and garlic; drizzle with 1 tbsp (15 mL) olive oil, toss to combine and then spread in a single layer. Bake for 20 minutes. Remove from oven.

4 Pat fish dry with paper towels and place on roasted vegetables; sprinkle with salt and pepper and drizzle remaining olive oil over top. Scatter olives around the fish. Bake for 10 minutes or until fish flakes easily when tested. Garnish with parsley and fennel fronds.

TIPS

Other white fish you could use instead of the cod are haddock, tilapia or basa.

Fennel is sometimes sold with the fronds, the wispy leaves that look like dill, still attached. The fronds can be used as an herb to garnish the finished dish. The tough stalks can be used to add to soup or stock.

SHRIMP SAGANAKI

SERVES 6 · · ·

This Greek-style dish combines shrimp with tomatoes and feta and makes for a quick and easy meal. Set your trivet on the table and serve this meal right out of the skillet along with crusty bread to soak up all the sauce. Add a fresh green salad or your favorite vegetable for a delicious meal.

3 tbsp (45 mL) extra virgin olive oil

1 onion, finely chopped

1 can (28 oz/796 mL) diced tomatoes

5 garlic cloves, chopped

1 tsp (5 mL) granulated sugar

1 tsp (5 mL) salt

1 tsp (5 mL) dried oregano

1/4 tsp (2 mL) hot pepper flakes

1/4 tsp (1 mL) black pepper

1/3 cup (75 mL) sliced black olives

1 1/2 lbs (750 g) large raw shrimp, peeled and deveined

1 cup (250 mL) crumbled feta cheese

2 tbsp (30 mL) chopped fresh parsley or green onions

1 Place one oven rack in the middle position and another about 5 inches (12.5 cm) below the broiler. Preheat oven to 400°F (200°C).

2 In a large ovenproof skillet, heat oil over medium-high heat and add onion; cook, stirring occasionally, for 5 minutes. Add tomatoes, garlic, sugar, salt, oregano, hot pepper flakes and black pepper; bring to a boil. Reduce heat to medium and cook uncovered for 8 to 10 minutes, until mixture is reduced by half, stirring occasionally.

3 Remove skillet from heat, sprinkle with olives and arrange shrimp on top in a single layer. Bake on middle rack for 5 minutes or until shrimp is almost cooked through; the flesh will begin to turn white with pink undertones and just begin to curl into a C shape.

4 Remove skillet from oven and turn on broiler. Sprinkle feta on top of shrimp and broil 1 to 2 minutes until feta is lightly browned. Sprinkle parsley on top just before serving.

TIPS

If you only have small shrimp, reduce bake time by a couple of minutes.

If using frozen shrimp, thaw thoroughly in the fridge, drain well and pat dry before cooking.

As an option, serve with pita bread instead of crusty bread.

CAJUN SHRIMP

SERVES 4 TO 6 · 🕐 30

Spicy Cajun flavors kick up this easy cream sauce,
which adds smoothness to the heat of the dish. Be sure to
serve it over rice or noodles to absorb all the sauce.

1 lb (500 g) large raw
shrimp, peeled and
deveined

1 tsp (5 mL) smoked
paprika

1 smoked sausage (about
4 oz/125 g total), thinly
sliced

1 tbsp (15 mL) all-purpose
flour

1 cup (250 mL) half-and-
half (10%) cream

½ cup (125 mL) ready-
to-use reduced-sodium
vegetable or chicken
broth

3 garlic cloves, minced

½ tsp (2 mL) dried thyme

¼ tsp (1 mL) cayenne
pepper

1 green onion, thinly sliced

1 In a bowl, toss shrimp and paprika together to coat;
set aside.

2 In a large nonstick skillet, fry sausage slices for
about 4 minutes or until golden; remove to plate. In
a small bowl, whisk flour into cream and add broth.

3 Return skillet to medium-high heat and add cream
mixture, garlic, thyme and cayenne pepper. Bring to
a boil and add shrimp; simmer for about 4 minutes
or until shrimp is pink and firm. Return sausage to
skillet and warm through. Serve in shallow bowls and
sprinkle with green onion.

TIP

Large shrimp is labeled 31/35, meaning there are
31 to 35 shrimp in each pound.

If the smoked sausages are spicy, reduce the
cayenne pepper to ⅛ tsp (0.5 mL).

SALMON CHICKPEA LOAF

SERVES 4 TO 5

Canned salmon is one of our favorite pantry staples because it's so versatile. We've added a "secret" ingredient of mashed chickpeas. Serve this tasty weeknight meal with a green salad and our Lemony Roasted Potatoes with Olives (page 178) or Zucchini Ribbons with Edamame (page 184).

1 cup (250 mL) cooked chickpeas

2 cans (8 oz/213 g each) sockeye salmon, drained

2 large eggs

1 cup (250 mL) milk

1½ cups (375 mL) panko bread crumbs

1 onion, finely chopped

1 dill pickle, finely chopped

1 tbsp (15 mL) lemon juice

2 tsp (10 mL) lemon zest

2 tsp (10 mL) dried dill

1 tsp (5 mL) salt

½ tsp (2 mL) black pepper

½ tsp (2 mL) garlic powder

1 Preheat oven to 350°F (180°C). Spray a 9- by 5-inch (23 by 12.5 cm) loaf pan with nonstick cooking spray.

2 In a large bowl, mash chickpeas using a potato masher or a fork. Add salmon and mash together. Add eggs and milk; stir to combine. Add panko, onion, dill pickle, lemon juice, lemon zest, dill, salt, pepper and garlic powder; stir until well combined.

3 Scrape the salmon mixture into the prepared pan. Use a spatula to smooth and pack down firmly.

Bake for 50 to 55 minutes until firm and the edges are golden. (An inserted small knife in the center should feel hot to the touch.) Let cool 10 minutes before slicing and serving.

TIPS

Serve with a sauce if you like. Tartar sauce, sour cream, plain Greek yogurt or ranch dressing would all be tasty options.

Make this dairy-free by using milk alternatives such as oat, almond or soy milk.

SKILLET GNOCCHI AND SHRIMP

SERVES 4 · · ·

Sun-dried tomato pesto brings the flavor of summer to this simple skillet meal and makes it easy to get on the table on a busy fall night.

2 tbsp (30 mL) extra virgin olive oil

1 package (12.5 oz/350 g) potato gnocchi

1 bag (12 oz/340 g) raw large black tiger shrimp, thawed, peeled and deveined

1 small zucchini, sliced into half moons

¼ tsp (1 mL) each salt and black pepper

⅓ cup (75 mL) sun-dried tomato pesto

1 In a large nonstick skillet, heat oil over medium-high heat. Add gnocchi and sauté for about 5 minutes or until golden. Remove with a slotted spoon to a bowl.

2 Return skillet to medium-high heat and sauté shrimp, zucchini, salt and pepper for about 5 minutes or until shrimp are pink and zucchini is golden. Reduce heat to medium and stir in gnocchi and pesto. Cook, stirring frequently, for about 2 minutes or until gnocchi are heated through.

What do shrimp wear in the kitchen? A-prawns.

SHEET-PAN FISH TACOS

SERVES 4 · (30) · [ ]

Fish pieces are first coated in a mayonnaise mixture then rolled in a seasoned panko mixture for fantastic flavor. Fish tacos are a big hit with Sylvia's family. They enjoy eating this slightly messy meal with plenty of hot sauce and pickled jalapeños.

1 lb (500 g) cod fillets

1 cup (250 mL) panko bread crumbs

1 tsp (2 mL) chili powder

1/2 tsp (2 mL) garlic powder

1/2 tsp (2 mL) ground cumin

1/2 tsp (2 mL) salt

1/2 cup (125 mL) mayonnaise

2 tsp (10 mL) smoked paprika

Canola oil for drizzling

8 small corn or flour tortillas

2 cups (500 mL) finely shredded cabbage

1/4 cup (60 mL) chopped cilantro

1 green onion, chopped

TOPPINGS

Lime wedges

Crumbled feta cheese

Chopped red onion

Avocado slices or prepared guacamole

1 Preheat oven to 425°F (220°C). Lightly oil a large rimmed baking sheet.

2 Pat fish dry with paper towels and cut into 2-inch (5 cm) pieces.

3 In a shallow dish, add panko, chili powder, garlic powder, cumin and salt; stir to combine. In a bowl, combine mayonnaise and smoked paprika; set aside 2 tbsp (30 mL) of the mixture for later. Toss fish in mayonnaise mixture, then roll in crumb mixture, pressing gently so the fish is evenly coated. Place on prepared baking sheet, making sure the fish are not overcrowded; drizzle a little extra oil on top of the fish pieces. Bake fish for 12 minutes or until fish is golden and flakes when tested with a fork. Meanwhile, stack and wrap tortillas in foil, place in oven for the last 6 minutes of baking.

4 Combine the remaining mayonnaise mixture with cabbage, cilantro and green onion.

5 Divide fish and cabbage mixture among tortillas. Top each with some lime juice, cheese, red onion and avocado. Serve right away.

TIP

The cod can be substituted with other white fish such as basa, tilapia, haddock or pollock.

STUFFED TROUT WITH LEMON PARSLEY BUTTER

SERVES 4 ·

Using fun dips with tons of flavor is an easy way to jazz up your regular fish dishes. If you can't find trout, no worries — use fillets of other fish such as sole, cod or tilapia.

4 trout fillets, skinless

1 tsp (5 mL) Montreal steak spice

1 cup (250 mL) artichoke and asiago dip

1 small shallot, finely diced

1 small red bell pepper, diced

1/4 cup (60 mL) butter, melted

1/2 tsp (2 mL) grated lemon zest

2 tbsp (30 mL) chopped fresh parsley

1. Preheat oven to 425°F (220°C). Line a baking sheet with parchment paper.

2. Sprinkle trout fillets with steak spice all over and place 2 on prepared baking sheet. Divide and spread artichoke and asiago dip on the 2 fillets. Sprinkle with shallot and red pepper. Place remaining 2 trout fillets on top and press together gently.

3. Whisk together butter, parsley and lemon zest. Spoon over top of trout fillets and bake for about 15 minutes or until trout flakes when tested with a fork.

4. Cut each stuffed trout in half to serve.

TIP

If your trout fillets are large, you will need only 2; cut them in half to put them together.

SEARED SALMON WITH CURRY YOGURT SAUCE

SERVES 4 · · · ·

Seared salmon with crispy skin tastes so good with the flavorful curry sauce and the fresh herb and onion topping. Serve with a side salad or with sautéed vegetables.

SALMON

2 tbsp (30 mL) canola oil

4 skin-on salmon fillets
(about 6 oz/175 g each)

½ tsp (2 mL) salt

¼ tsp (1 mL) black pepper

YOGURT SAUCE

¼ cup (60 mL) full-fat
plain yogurt

2 tbsp (30 mL) mayonnaise

1 tsp (5 mL) lime zest

1 tsp (5 mL) lime juice

1 tsp (5 mL) curry powder

2 tbsp (30 mL) chopped
cilantro

1 tbsp (15 mL) finely
chopped red onion

1 SALMON: In a nonstick skillet, heat oil over medium-high heat. Pat the fish dry with paper towels and sprinkle with salt and pepper. Cook salmon skin-side up, without moving the fillets, about 4 minutes until golden.

2 YOGURT SAUCE: Meanwhile, in a small bowl, combine yogurt, mayonnaise, lime zest, lime juice and curry powder. Season with extra salt and pepper to taste.

3 Flip fish over, skin-side down and reduce heat to medium. Cook another 3 to 4 minutes, until skin is crisp and fish is cooked to desired doneness.

4 Transfer to serving plates, drizzle with yogurt sauce and sprinkle with cilantro and onion.

TIPS

Choose fillets that are the same thickness for even cooking.

Allow the salmon to sit at room temperature for about 10 minutes before cooking.

MAKE AHEAD

The yogurt sauce can be made a day ahead. Refrigerate in an airtight container

CANNED TUNA BOWL

SERVES 2 ·

This fresh and colorful tuna bowl is wonderful for lunch or dinner — enjoy warm or cold! Make the bowl ahead and tuck it in the fridge for a cool dinner on the patio.

1 tbsp (15 mL) canola oil

1 small onion, diced

2 garlic cloves, minced

1 cup (250 mL) basmati rice

2 cups (500 mL) ready-to-use vegetable broth

1 carrot, shredded

2 tbsp (30 mL) chopped fresh parsley

1 can (6 oz/170 g) chunk light tuna in water, drained

1 cup (250 mL) grape tomatoes, halved

1 cup (250 mL) diced cucumber

1/2 cup (125 mL) chopped fresh cilantro

Salt and black pepper

2 lime wedges

1 In a saucepan, heat oil over medium heat. Cook onion and garlic for about 3 minutes or until softened. Stir in basmati to coat. Add broth and bring to a boil. Cover and reduce heat to low; cook for about 15 minutes or until rice is tender and broth is absorbed. Fluff with fork and stir in carrot and parsley.

2 Divide between two bowls and top with tuna, tomatoes, cucumber and cilantro. Sprinkle with salt and pepper to taste. Squeeze lime wedge over top before enjoying.

TIP

Use more lime if you want to add a bit more zip to your tuna bowl.

VEGETARIAN

~

CHEESY CORN PIZZA

SERVES 4 ·  ·

If you're craving cheesy pizza, this one is quick and easy to assemble. Using pita bread as the base means a thin crispy crust under the ooey gooey cheese and corn topping. The pizza is delicious as is, but we also enjoy it drizzled with hot honey.

4 7-inch (18 cm) pitas

1/4 cup (50 mL) ranch dressing, plus extra for serving

2 green onions, chopped

1 tsp (5 mL) hot pepper flakes

Pinch salt

1 cup (250 mL) grated mozzarella cheese

1 cup (250 mL) grated Cheddar cheese

1 cup (250 mL) frozen corn kernels, thawed and well drained

1 cup (250 mL) grated Parmesan cheese

1 cup (250 mL) baby spinach or arugula (optional)

1 Preheat oven to 450°F (230°C). Arrange pitas in a single layer on a large rimmed baking sheet.

2 Divide and spread the dressing onto the pitas, then evenly divide and sprinkle green onion, hot pepper flakes, salt, mozzarella cheese, Cheddar cheese, corn and then Parmesan onto each pita.

3 Bake 6 to 8 minutes, or until the pita is crisp on the bottom. Remove from oven and divide the spinach, if using, onto each pita. Serve with extra ranch dressing and hot pepper flakes on the side.

TIP

Grated aged Pecorino Romano or Grano Padano cheese can substitute for the Parmesan cheese.

CREAMY MUSHROOM AND LENTIL ORZO

SERVES 4 · 30 · ·

This easy one-pot meal is creamy, rich and satisfying. Using a variety of mushrooms will give this dish extra flavor.

3 tbsp (45 mL) canola oil

1 onion, finely chopped

1½ lbs (750 g) assorted mushrooms, sliced

1 large carrot, coarsely grated

2 garlic cloves, minced

2 tsp (10 mL) chopped fresh thyme

1 tsp (5 mL) balsamic vinegar

1 tsp (5 mL) salt

½ tsp (2 mL) black pepper

2 cups (500 mL) ready-to-use vegetable broth

1 can (19 oz/540 mL) lentils, rinsed and drained

1½ cups (375 mL) orzo pasta

2 cups (500 mL) milk

¾ cup (175 mL) grated Parmesan cheese

1 In a large nonstick skillet or pot, heat oil over medium-high heat, add onions; cook 3 minutes, stirring occasionally. Stir in mushrooms, carrot, garlic, thyme, vinegar, salt and pepper; cook 2 minutes, stirring occasionally. Add broth, lentils, orzo and milk; bring to a boil. Reduce heat to medium; cook uncovered, stirring frequently to keep the orzo from sticking to the bottom of the pot. Cook 10 minutes or until the orzo is tender. Mixture should be creamy, so add a splash more milk, broth or water as needed.

2 Ladle into bowls and sprinkle each with Parmesan cheese.

TIPS

Pecorino cheese can be substituted for the Parmesan cheese.

To make this vegan, substitute non-dairy milk for the milk and vegan Parmesan for the Parmesan.

EASY ONE-POT PASTA

SERVES 6 ·

Here's a delicious version of a comfort food classic, a popular boxed pasta mix. Sylvia's meat-loving friend gave this dish two thumbs up! Serve with a fresh green salad or your favorite vegetable on the side.

3 tbsp (45 mL) canola oil

1 onion, diced

2 cups (500 mL) chopped mushrooms

1 package (12 oz/340 g) veggie ground round (ground soy)

4 garlic cloves, minced

2 tsp (10 mL) dried Italian seasoning

1 tsp (5 mL) smoked paprika

1/2 tsp (2 mL) each salt and black pepper

1 can (28 oz/796 mL) diced tomatoes

1 1/2 cups (375 mL) ready-to-use vegetable broth

2 tbsp (30 mL) soy sauce or tamari

2 cups (500 ml) dried elbow macaroni pasta

1 In a large pot, heat oil over medium-high heat. Add onion and cook, stirring occasionally, for 7 minutes or until onion begins to turn golden brown. Add mushrooms and cook, stirring for 2 minutes. Reduce heat to medium and add ground round, garlic, Italian seasoning, smoked paprika, salt and pepper, breaking up ground round with a spoon; cook for 1 minute.

2 Add tomatoes, broth and soy sauce; bring to a simmer and cook for 5 minutes, stirring occasionally. Add macaroni; stir to combine. Cover and simmer, stirring occasionally, scraping up any sticking food from the bottom of pot. Cook for 15 to 20 minutes or until macaroni is tender, stirring occasionally.

TIP
Other short pasta such as penne, fusilli or cavatappi can be used in place of the macaroni.

SWEET AND SPICY CAULIFLOWER AND CHICKPEAS

SERVES 4 ·

We start by browning one side of the cauliflower on the stovetop, then it's baked with chickpeas until golden and crisp on the outside. The dish is finished with a bright and flavorful sauce and given added crunch with sesame seeds.

2 tbsp (30 mL) canola oil, divided

1 (1 lb/500g) head cauliflower, cut into 4 wedges

1/2 tsp (2 mL) salt, divided

1 can (19 oz/540 mL) chickpeas, rinsed, drained and patted dry with paper towel

2 tsp (10 mL) honey

2 tsp (10 mL) ketchup

2 tsp (10 mL) soy sauce

1 1/2 tsp (7 mL) chili garlic sauce

1 tsp (5 mL) cider vinegar

2 tsp (10 mL) toasted sesame seeds

1 green onion, thinly sliced

1 Preheat oven to 425°F (220°C).

2 In a heavy ovenproof skillet, heat 1 tbsp (15 mL) oil over medium-high heat. Place cauliflower wedges cut side down and sprinkle with half the salt. Cook cauliflower without moving it for 7 minutes or until golden brown on the bottom, then flip pieces over. Sprinkle chickpeas around the cauliflower, drizzle with remaining oil, then sprinkle with remaining salt. Place skillet in oven and bake 25 minutes or until the cauliflower is tender.

3 Meanwhile, in a small bowl, whisk together honey, ketchup, soy sauce, chili garlic sauce and vinegar.

4 Remove skillet from oven and transfer cauliflower and chickpeas to a serving plate. Drizzle half of the sauce over top. Sprinkle with sesame seeds and green onion and serve remaining sauce on the side for dipping.

TIP

There's no need to trim the leaves off the cauliflower, but do remove some of the tough stem. The leaves become wonderfully crisp in the oven.

SKILLET VEGETABLE POT PIE

SERVES 6 · 🍲 · 🌱

Frozen puff pastry is one of our favorite shortcut ingredients.
This pie is perfect for a weekend brunch or a weeknight meal.
Serve with a fresh green salad or our Beet, Citrus and
Pear Salad (see page 57).

½ package (1 lb/450 g) frozen puff pastry sheets, thawed

3 tbsp (45 mL) canola oil

1 onion, finely chopped

2 carrots, diced

2 celery stalks, diced

5 cups (1.25 L) sliced mushrooms

1 garlic clove, minced

3 tbsp (45 mL) all-purpose flour

1 tsp (5 mL) dried Italian seasoning

½ tsp (2 mL) each salt and black pepper

1 cup (250 mL) half-and-half (10%) cream, divided

1½ cups (375 mL) ready-to-use vegetable broth

1 tbsp (15 mL) soy sauce

1 can (19 oz/540 mL) lentils, rinsed and drained

½ cup (125 mL) frozen peas

1 Preheat oven to 425°F (220°C).

2 On a lightly floured surface, roll and trim the pastry to create a 10-inch (25 cm) circle; cover and refrigerate until ready to use.

3 In a 10-inch (25 cm) ovenproof skillet, heat oil over medium-high heat. Add onion, carrots and celery; cook 5 minutes, stirring occasionally, until vegetables begin to soften. Add mushrooms and garlic; cook 5 minutes, stirring occasionally. Reduce heat to medium and sprinkle the flour, Italian seasoning, salt and pepper over top; stir to combine and cook 2 minutes, stirring occasionally. Gradually stir in all but 1 tsp (5 mL) of the cream; cook and stir until mixture begins to thicken, about 2 minutes. Gradually add the broth and soy sauce; bring to a simmer and cook until mixture is thick and creamy, about 5 minutes, stirring frequently. Remove from heat; stir in lentils and peas until well combined.

4 Carefully place pastry on top of warm vegetable mixture; brush the top with remaining 1 tsp (5 mL) cream. Use a sharp knife to cut a few vent holes in the pastry for steam to escape. Bake 30 minutes, or until pastry is golden brown. Remove from oven and let cool a few minutes before serving.

TIPS

To make this vegan, use vegetable-based puff pastry and coconut milk in place of the cream.

Use a variety of mushrooms in this recipe. When buying, look for mushrooms that are plump and firm.

TOFU PUTTANESCA

SERVES 4 · 🥘 · 🌿

The traditional puttanesca, a classic intensely tasty Italian sauce usually served with pasta, makes a quick weeknight meal. The rich flavors of capers, olives and hot pepper enliven the tomatoes and tofu and create a hearty vegetarian meal when poured over a bed of couscous. The tofu breaks apart slightly in the sauce and absorbs all the flavors.

2 tbsp (30 mL) extra virgin olive oil

1 small onion, diced

3 garlic cloves, minced

1/2 tsp (2 mL) hot pepper flakes

1 can (19 oz/540 mL) petite-cut stewed tomatoes

1 1/2 cups (375 mL) diced firm tofu

1/4 cup (60 mL) chopped, pitted, sun-dried olives

2 tbsp (30 mL) chopped fresh oregano

2 tbsp (30 mL) chopped fresh Italian parsley

1 tbsp (15 mL) capers

Pinch salt

3 cups (750 mL) cooked couscous

1/4 cup (60 mL) grated Parmesan cheese

1. In a shallow saucepan, heat oil over medium heat. Cook onion, garlic and hot pepper flakes for about 3 minutes or until softened. Add tomatoes, tofu, olives, oregano, parsley, capers and salt and bring to a boil. Reduce heat and simmer for about 15 minutes or until thickened. Spoon over couscous and sprinkle with Parmesan before serving.

HOW TO MAKE COUSCOUS

In a saucepan, bring 1 cup (250 mL) ready-to-use vegetable broth or water to boil. Add 1 cup (250 mL) couscous and remove from heat. Cover and let stand for 10 minutes. Fluff with fork before serving. Add salt and pepper to taste.

SKILLET LASAGNA

SERVES 4 TO 6 ·

Take your lasagna to the skillet with this rustic deconstructed lasagna. A rich sauce is created with the help of ricotta and mozzarella cheeses. Dinner is ready!

4 sheets fresh pasta

1 tbsp (15 mL) canola oil

3 garlic cloves, minced

1 onion, diced

1 tbsp (15 mL) dried oregano

$\frac{1}{2}$ tsp (2 mL) salt

$\frac{1}{4}$ tsp (1 mL) hot pepper flakes

1 can (19 oz/540 mL) petite-cut stewed tomatoes, with juice

1 cup (250 mL) ready-to-use vegetable broth

4 cups (1 L) lightly packed baby spinach

1 cup (250 mL) ricotta cheese

$\frac{3}{4}$ cup (175 mL) shredded mozzarella cheese

3 tbsp (45 mL) chopped fresh basil or parsley

1. Cut pasta sheets in half crosswise, then cut into $1\frac{1}{2}$ inch (3 cm) wide strips; set aside.

2. In a large, deep nonstick skillet, heat oil over medium heat. Cook garlic and onion for 3 minutes or until softened. Add oregano, salt and hot pepper flakes; cook, stirring for 1 minute.

3. Add tomatoes and broth to skillet; bring to a boil. Stir in spinach and pasta; return to simmer. Cover and cook for about 8 minutes or until pasta is tender. Uncover, dollop with ricotta and sprinkle with mozzarella cheese; cook for about 2 minutes to heat ricotta and melt mozzarella. Sprinkle with basil.

FETA AND KALE-STUFFED MUSHROOMS

SERVES 6 ·

For the avid grillers, these mushrooms can be cooked
on your outdoor grill to add a smoky flavor.

10 portobello mushrooms
(about 4 inches/10 cm in
diameter), divided

1 tbsp (15 mL) canola oil

1 onion, finely chopped

4 garlic cloves, minced

1/2 tsp (2 mL) salt

6 cups (1.5 L) lightly
packed fresh baby kale,
chopped, or chopped
Swiss chard

3 tbsp (45 mL) chopped
fresh dill

1 cup (250 mL) crumbled
feta cheese

1/3 cup (75 mL) seasoned
dry bread crumbs

1 Remove stems from the mushrooms and chop
finely. Using a small spoon, scrape out the dark
gills of the mushroom caps and discard. Place 6 of
the mushroom caps aside. Finely chop remaining
4 mushrooms and add to chopped stems.

2 Preheat oven to 400°F (200°C).

3 In a large ovenproof nonstick skillet, heat oil over
medium-high heat; add onion, garlic and chopped
mushrooms, stems and salt and cook for about
8 minutes or until softened and golden. Stir in kale
and dill; cook for about 4 minutes or until wilted. Stir
in feta and bread crumbs to combine.

4 Spoon mixture into mushrooms caps. Place stuffed
caps back into skillet. Bake for about 18 minutes or
until mushrooms are tender and cheese is golden.

TIP
Make these mushrooms ahead of time by preparing
them and refrigerating for up to 4 hours until you
are ready to bake them.

SKILLET RAPINI SAUSAGE PIZZA

SERVES 4

This poured pizza is made from a batter instead of a traditional pizza dough and resembles a flat bread or deep-dish pizza. Create your own topping creations once you try out our version.

2 tbsp (30 mL) canola oil

1/2 cup (125 mL) cornmeal

1 cup (250 mL) all-purpose flour

1 tsp (5 mL) baking powder

1/2 tsp (2 mL) salt

1/2 tsp (2 mL) Italian seasoning

2 large eggs

2/3 cup (150 mL) milk

1/3 cup (75 mL) pizza or pasta sauce

1 cup (250 mL) rapini, chopped and cooked

1 cooked plant-based sausage, sliced, or 1/2 cup (125 mL) sliced plant-based pepperoni

1 cup (250 mL) shredded mozzarella cheese

1 Drizzle oil in a 10-inch (25 cm) cast-iron skillet to coat. Sprinkle cornmeal all over skillet and place in cold oven. Preheat oven to 400°F (200°C).

2 In a blender, combine flour, baking powder, salt, Italian seasoning, eggs and milk. Blend on medium for about 2 minutes until smooth. Once oven temperature is reached, remove skillet with oven mitts and pour batter into skillet. Return skillet to oven and bake for about 15 minutes or until golden brown.

3 Spread base with pizza sauce and sprinkle with rapini and sausage. Sprinkle with cheese and return to oven for about 5 minutes or until cheese is melted. Let cool slightly before serving.

TIP
There is plenty of cornmeal in the skillet to make it easier to remove the pizza from the skillet and offer up some crunch as well.

POTATO PEPPER AND ZUCCHINI CASSEROLE

SERVES 6 TO 8 · ·

When vegetables are in season together, they taste amazing together. Just add some some crusty bread to enjoy a hearty vegetarian meal.

1½ lbs (750 g) mini potatoes, halved

2 small zucchini, sliced

2 red bell peppers, coarsely chopped

2 garlic cloves, minced

3 tbsp (45 mL) extra virgin olive oil

½ tsp (2 mL) each salt and black pepper

1 sprig fresh rosemary

2 cups (500 mL) grape tomatoes

3 tbsp (45 mL) chopped fresh basil or parsley

¾ cup (175 mL) crumbled feta cheese

1 Preheat oven to 425°F (220°C). Lightly spray a 13- by 9-inch (33 by 23 cm) casserole dish.

2 Combine potatoes, zucchini, red peppers and garlic in prepared casserole dish. Drizzle with oil, salt and pepper; toss to coat well. Place rosemary on top and roast for 30 minutes, stirring once.

3 Stir in tomatoes and basil. Sprinkle with feta and return to oven for about 15 minutes or until tomatoes are blistered and vegetables are golden and tender.

TIP
Make this vegan by using a vegan feta-style cheese.

What does a vegetable wear to the beach? A zucchini.

SPINACH RICOTTA-STUFFED SQUASH

SERVES 2 TO 4 · 🌾 · 🌿

Enjoy this as a hearty vegetarian meal or cut it smaller to serve as a side dish option. However you serve it, you will love it!

2 acorn squash (about 2 lbs/1 kg each)

1/2 tsp each salt and pepper, divided

1/2 cup (125 mL) ricotta cheese

1/2 cup (125 mL) table (18%) cream

1/4 cup (60 mL) basil pesto or sun-dried tomato pesto

2 garlic cloves, minced

1 1/2 tsp (7 mL) dried Italian seasoning

1 container (5 oz/142 g) baby spinach

2 cups (500 mL) shredded Gruyère cheese, divided

1 Preheat oven to 425°F (220°C). Line a large baking sheet with parchment paper.

2 Prick squash all over with tines of fork or sharp knife. Microwave for 3 minutes to soften. Cut each squash in half lengthwise. Scoop out seeds. Place squash halves, cut side up, on prepared sheet. Sprinkle with a pinch each of the salt and pepper.

3 Stir together ricotta, cream, pesto, garlic, Italian seasoning and remaining salt and pepper. Stir in spinach until well combined. Stir in half of the Gruyère.

4 Divide mixture evenly among the squash halves. Cover with foil. Bake for 30 minutes. Remove foil. Sprinkle with remaining Gruyère and bake for about 25 minutes or until squash is tender and cheese is melted and slightly golden. Let stand for 10 minutes before serving.

SIDES

～

LEMONY ROASTED POTATOES WITH OLIVES

SERVES 6 ·

We love potatoes! These are baked until crusty and browned with herbs and briny olives. The drizzle of lemon juice, zest and Parmesan cheese elevates the deliciousness of one of our favorite comfort foods.

2 lbs (1 kg) baby or small potatoes, cut in half

5 garlic cloves, smashed

3 tbsp (45 mL) canola oil

3/4 tsp (3 mL) salt

1/2 tsp (2 mL) dried rosemary

1/4 tsp (1 mL) black pepper

1/2 cup (125 mL) olives, pitted and sliced

2 tsp (10 mL) lemon juice

2 tsp (10 mL) lemon zest

2 tbsp (30 mL) grated Parmesan cheese

2 tbsp (30 mL) chopped fresh parsley

1 Preheat oven to 425°F (220°C).

2 Place potatoes and garlic on a rimmed baking sheet. Drizzle with oil, sprinkle with salt, rosemary and pepper, then toss to combine well. Arrange the potatoes in a single layer, cut side down. Bake 20 minutes, remove from oven, add olives and toss to combine. Bake another 25 to 35 minutes or until potatoes are tender.

3 Remove from oven and drizzle with lemon juice and lemon zest; toss to combine. Transfer to a serving platter and sprinkle with Parmesan cheese and parsley.

TIP

Many types of olives work in this recipe — use your favorite variety.

HONEY OAT BEER BREAD

SERVES 8 TO 10 ·

A hearty bread to serve with soup, chili or stew — not only does it take mere minutes to come together, it smells and tastes delicious.

2 cups (500 mL) all-purpose flour

³⁄₄ cup (175 mL) quick oats

1 tbsp (15 mL) baking powder

1 tsp (5 mL) salt

1 can (12 oz/354 mL) dark beer, room temperature

¹⁄₄ cup (60 mL) honey

¹⁄₄ cup (60 mL) melted butter, divided

1 Preheat oven to 375°F (190°C). Spray a 9- by 5-inch (23 by 12.5 cm) loaf pan with nonstick cooking spray or line with parchment paper.

2 In a large bowl, whisk together flour, oats, baking powder and salt until well combined. Pour in the beer, honey and half of the butter; mix until just combined. Spoon into prepared baking pan and smooth the top of the batter. Drizzle remaining melted butter on top.

3 Bake for 50 to 55 minutes, or until a tester inserted in the center comes out clean. Let cool in pan on a wire rack for 10 minutes, then transfer loaf to a wire rack to cool completely.

TIP

Store in an airtight container for up to 3 days. Or wrap well, store in a freezer-safe container and freeze for up to 3 months

HERBED HONEY OAT BEER BREAD

Add 2 tsp (10 mL) dried Italian seasoning to the dry ingredients.

CHEDDAR HONEY OAT BEER BREAD

Stir ¹⁄₂ cup (125 mL) grated sharp (old) Cheddar into the batter.

SMASHED MIXED POTATOES

SERVES 4 TO 6 · · ·

A colorful mix of crisp potatoes with a hint of maple sweetness makes these popular with the whole family and easy to serve alongside any of your favorite main courses!

2 sweet potatoes, scrubbed (about 1 lb/500 g)

3 yellow-fleshed potatoes, scrubbed (about 1 lb/500 g)

2 tbsp (30 mL) canola oil

2 tbsp (30 mL) chopped fresh parsley

2 tsp (10 mL) chopped fresh rosemary or thyme

$\frac{1}{2}$ tsp (2 mL) each salt and black pepper

3 tbsp (45 mL) butter, melted

2 tbsp (30 mL) maple syrup

1 Preheat oven to 425°F (220°C). Line a large baking sheet with parchment paper.

2 Cut both sweet and yellow-fleshed potatoes into 1-inch (2.5 cm) thick rounds and place on prepared sheet. Drizzle with oil and sprinkle with parsley, rosemary, salt and pepper. Toss gently to coat evenly and make sure all the slices lie flat in a single layer. Roast for 20 minutes. Turn over and roast for about 10 minutes or until golden brown and tender.

3 Meanwhile, whisk together butter and maple syrup; set aside.

4 Using a fork, gently smash the potatoes and drizzle all over with butter mixture. Return to oven for 5 minutes.

STICKY RICE WITH NAPA CABBAGE

SERVES 6 TO 8 · · ·

Shake up your usual cabbage with this mixture of mushrooms and rice for a perfect accompaniment to serve alongside your favorite roast.

3 tbsp (45 mL) canola oil

12 oz (375 g) shiitake mushrooms, sliced

4 green onions, thinly sliced

3 garlic cloves, minced

1 tbsp (15 mL) minced fresh ginger

5 cups (1.25 L) sliced Napa cabbage

1 red bell pepper, thinly sliced

3 cups (750 mL) hot cooked sticky rice (see instructions)

3 tbsp (45 mL) soy sauce

3 tbsp (45 mL) rice vinegar

1 In a large nonstick skillet, heat oil over medium heat and cook mushrooms, onions, garlic and ginger for 5 minutes or until softened. Stir in cabbage and red pepper and cook for about 5 minutes or until wilted but tender crisp.

2 Spread rice out into large shallow dish and add Napa cabbage mixture. Drizzle with soy sauce and vinegar and toss to combine.

TO COOK STICKY RICE

You can use any leftover cooked rice for this recipe but if you need to cook some up, here are instructions. In a saucepan, bring 1 cup (250 mL) Calrose (sushi) rice and 2 cups (500 mL) ready-to-use vegetable or chicken broth to boil. Reduce heat, cover and cook for about 20 minutes or until broth is absorbed.

ZUCCHINI RIBBONS WITH EDAMAME

SERVES 4

This side dish is a perfect way to use up zucchini when it's in season. You can add an extra pop of color by using a combination of yellow and green zucchini.

1 tbsp (15 mL) olive oil

1 large shallot, thinly sliced

1 lb (500 g) small zucchini, sliced into thin ribbons

2 cups (500 mL) frozen edamame beans, thawed and drained

1/4 tsp (1 mL) garlic powder

1 tbsp (15 mL) chopped fresh parsley

1 tsp (5 mL) lemon zest

Salt and black pepper

1 In a large skillet, heat oil over medium-high heat. Add shallot and cook for 2 minutes, stirring occasionally. Add zucchini, edamame and garlic powder; cook for 2 to 3 minutes, using tongs to toss occasionally until zucchini is tender crisp. Remove from heat; sprinkle with parsley and lemon zest. Season with salt and pepper to taste.

TIPS

Run a vegetable peeler down the length of the zucchini to create long ribbons. Peel until you reach the center seed portion, then flip the zucchini over and continue peeling on each side. You can also use a mandoline.

Look for firm, smaller zucchini for the best flavor.

ROASTED BRUSSELS SPROUTS AND PARSNIPS

SERVES 4 TO 6 ·

Late harvest vegetables take on a complex sweetness when drizzled with extra virgin olive oil and aged balsamic vinegar. Roasting the vegetables gives them a tender-crisp texture that makes them ideal for serving alongside any roast.

1 lb (500 g) Brussels sprouts, halved

1 lb (500 g) parsnips, peeled and sliced

2 garlic cloves, minced

1/4 cup (60 mL) extra virgin olive oil, divided

1/2 tsp (2 mL) each salt and black pepper

2 tbsp (30 mL) aged balsamic vinegar

2 tbsp (30 mL) chopped fresh parsley

1 Preheat oven to 400°F (200°C). Line a baking sheet with parchment paper.

2 Spread Brussels sprouts, parsnips and garlic on prepared sheet. Drizzle with 3 tbsp (45 mL) of the oil, salt and pepper. Toss together to coat. Roast for about 30 minutes or until tender and golden brown.

3 Scrape into a serving bowl and drizzle with vinegar, remaining oil and parsley to serve.

TIP

This veggie mix can be made up to 2 days ahead and warmed up in the microwave or oven. They are just as delicious cold served up as a salad.

BLACK BEAN SALSA

SERVES 4 TO 6 · · ·

This refreshing salsa is an excellent accompaniment
for any grilled meats or fish. You can also enjoy it on
its own with tortilla chips or crisp pita wedges.

2 cans (19 oz/540 mL
each) black beans,
drained and rinsed

½ cup (125 mL) diced
tomatoes

⅓ cup (75 mL) chopped
fresh cilantro

¼ cup (60 mL) diced red
onion

1 jalapeño pepper, seeded
and diced

2 garlic cloves, minced

½ tsp (2 mL) grated lime
zest

2 tbsp (30 mL) lime juice

2 tbsp (30 mL) canola oil

½ tsp (2 mL) salt

1 In a large bowl, stir together beans, tomatoes,
cilantro, onion, jalapeño, garlic, lime zest, lime juice,
oil and salt. Let stand 10 minutes before serving.

TIP

Cover and refrigerate for up to 3 days. Stir well
and reseason if necessary.

Cilantro lovers unite! If you love that fresh herb
flavor, add double the amount of cilantro.

MANGO VARIATION

Peel, pit and dice 1 fresh ripe mango and stir into
the black bean salsa. Adjust lime juice and salt to
your taste.

CORN VARIATION

Stir 1 cup (250 mL) fresh corn kernels or thawed
frozen kernels into the black bean salsa. Adjust
lime juice and salt to your taste.

What kind of triangle is a tortilla chip?
An i-salsa-les triangle.

PARMESAN PEA ORZO

SERVES 6 · 🌱 · ⏱30 · 🍲

This one-pot creamy side dish goes with anything. But we've got to admit that eating it out of the pot on its own is okay too.

~~~~~~

1 tbsp (15 mL) butter

1 small onion, diced

2 garlic cloves, minced

1 cup (250 mL) orzo pasta

2 cups (500 mL) ready-to-use vegetable broth

1 cup (250 mL) frozen peas, thawed

½ cup (125 mL) grated Parmesan cheese

⅓ cup (75 mL) full-fat herb and garlic cream cheese

2 tbsp (30 mL) chopped fresh basil or parsley

1 In a saucepan, melt butter over medium heat and cook onion and garlic for about 3 minutes or until softened. Stir in orzo to coat. Add broth and bring to a boil. Reduce heat and simmer for about 8 minutes or until orzo is tender but firm. Stir in peas, Parmesan, cream cheese and basil; remove from heat. Cover and let stand for 5 minutes or until cheese is melted.

2 Stir well before serving. Sprinkle with more chopped basil if desired.

CURRIED ORZO

SERVES 6 TO 8 ·

Chickpeas add a nutty buttery element to this creamy and
flavorful pasta side dish. Serve alongside chicken, pork or beef.
Another option is to make a meatless meal and enjoy the orzo
with a platter of assorted grilled or roasted vegetables.

3 tbsp (45 mL) canola oil

1 onion, finely diced

1 celery stalk, diced

1 large carrot, finely diced

2 garlic cloves, minced

1 tbsp (15 mL) curry powder

1 tsp (5 mL) chili powder

1 tsp (5 mL) grated fresh
 ginger

1 tsp (5 mL) salt

$1/2$ tsp (2 mL) ground cumin

$1/2$ tsp (2 mL) ground
 coriander

$1^1/2$ cups (375 mL) orzo
 pasta

1 can (19 oz/540 mL)
 chickpeas, rinsed and
 drained

5 cups (1.25 L) ready-to-
 use chicken broth

$1/2$ cup (125 mL) chopped
 cilantro leaves and stems

1 In a large skillet, heat oil over medium-high heat.
   Add onion and cook 3 minutes, stirring occasionally.
   Add celery, carrot, garlic, curry powder, chili
   powder, ginger, salt, cumin and coriander and cook
   for 2 minutes, stirring occasionally. Stir in orzo and
   chickpeas, then add the broth and stir. Bring to a
   boil, cover and reduce heat to medium.

2 Stir occasionally until orzo is tender, about
   15 minutes. If mixture becomes dry, add a little more
   water to maintain a creamy texture. Stir in cilantro
   just before serving.

ZUCCHINI SKILLET CORNBREAD

SERVES 8 TO 10 ·

Zucchini gives this bread a moist texture — no dry, crumbly cornbread here! Slightly sweet with a hint of heat from the jalapeño and saltiness from the Cheddar, this is a delicious side dish you can serve at dinner or breakfast.

1 cup (250 mL) all-purpose flour

1 cup (250 mL) cornmeal

1 tbsp (15 mL) baking powder

1 1/2 tsp (7 mL) salt

3 large eggs

1 cup (250 mL) buttermilk

1/4 cup (60 mL) canola oil

1/4 cup (60 mL) packed light brown sugar

1 medium zucchini, grated (about 8 oz/250 g)

1 cup (250 mL) grated Cheddar cheese

2 green onions, chopped

1 jalapeño pepper, seeded and finely diced

1 Preheat oven to 400°F (200°C). Generously oil a 10-inch (25 cm) cast-iron skillet.

2 In a large bowl, whisk together flour, cornmeal, baking powder and salt until well combined. In another bowl, whisk together eggs, buttermilk, oil and sugar; then stir in zucchini, cheese, green onions and jalapeño. Stir wet mixture into cornmeal mixture until just combined.

3 Pour batter into skillet; bake for 25 to 30 minutes or until light golden brown and a tester inserted in the center comes out clean. Let cool on a wire rack for 10 minutes before serving.

TIPS

If desired, substitute whole wheat flour for half of the all-purpose flour.

Cornbread freezes well. Once completely cooled, wrap individual portions with plastic wrap and store in an airtight freezer container for up to 2 months.

SWEETS

~

PEACHES 'N' CREAM TART

SERVES 6 TO 8 ·

This tart is light and airy with a fresh summer, cinnamon-enhanced flavor of peaches and cream. The added sour cream keeps this dessert from being too sweet. Look for a prepared graham cracker pie crust in the baking aisle of your grocery store.

1 can (14 oz/398 mL) peach slices in fruit juice, drained

1 cup (250 mL) heavy or whipping (35%) cream

3 tbsp (45 mL) confectioners' (icing) sugar

3/4 cup (175 mL) sour cream

1/2 tsp (2 mL) vanilla

1/4 tsp (1 mL) ground cinnamon

1 9-inch (23 cm) graham cracker pie crust

Fresh mint leaves (optional)

1 Chop peaches into bite-size pieces and set aside on paper towel lined plate.

2 In a large bowl, whip cream and sugar until stiff peaks form. Whisk in sour cream, vanilla and cinnamon. Fold in peaches.

3 Scrape peach mixture into graham cracker crust and spread evenly, smoothing top. Refrigerate pie for at least 2 hours or until set.

4 Using a long knife dipped in hot water, cut tart and garnish with fresh mint leaves, if using.

TIPS

Use a chocolate graham crust for a darker chocolate-flavored pie crust.

Substitute 3 fresh ripe peaches, peeled and pitted, for the can of peaches.

What do you call the time in between eating peaches? A pit-stop.

BANANA CARAMEL SNACK CAKE

SERVES 8 ·

A sweet and crunchy pecan and sugar topping makes this
cake especially delicious. Be sure to bake with ripe bananas
to get the best flavor and sweetness.

1/2 cup (125 mL) butter,
melted

3/4 cup (175 mL) packed
dark brown sugar

2 large eggs

2 tsp (10 mL) vanilla

1 cup (250 mL) very ripe
mashed banana (about 3)

1 3/4 (425 mL) cups
all-purpose flour

1/2 tsp (2 mL) baking soda

1/2 tsp (2 mL) salt

3 tbsp (45 mL) chopped
pecans

2 tbsp (30 mL) granulated
sugar

GARNISH

Vanilla ice cream

Caramel sauce

Toffee bits

Banana slices

1 Preheat oven to 350°F (180°C). Spray a 9-inch
(23 cm) square baking pan with nonstick cooking
spray or line with parchment paper.

2 In a bowl, whisk together butter, brown sugar,
eggs, vanilla and bananas until well combined. Sift
flour, baking soda and salt over top and stir until
combined. Pour into prepared pan and smooth the
top. Sprinkle pecans and sugar evenly on top.

3 Bake for 30 to 35 minutes or until a tester inserted
in the center comes out clean. Let cool in pan
for 20 minutes, then transfer to the rack to cool
completely.

4 GARNISH: Serve cake with a scoop of ice cream,
garnished with a drizzle of caramel sauce, a sprinkle
of toffee bits and fresh banana slices.

TIPS

Try whipped cream as a tasty option to serve with
this cake instead of ice cream.

Store in an airtight container at room temperature
for up to 2 days.

MANDARIN ORANGE YOGURT MOUSSE

SERVES 6 TO 8 ·

Light and refreshing, this dessert will brighten your day. Add some crumbled chocolate cookies or half a pizzelle cookie when serving. If you love chocolate and orange, then a sprinkle of chopped chocolate over top is perfect! Or try our Orange Candied Pecan Garnish for added crunch (see below).

1 tbsp (15 mL) grated orange zest

1/3 cup (75 mL) granulated sugar

3/4 cup (175 mL) heavy or whipping (35%) cream

2 cups (500 mL) 2% Greek-style vanilla yogurt

2 tbsp (30 mL) orange juice

1 tsp (5 mL) vanilla

2 cans (10 oz/284 mL each) mandarin oranges, drained

1 In a large bowl, with your fingers, rub together (or stir) orange zest and sugar until sugar is orange in color; remove half to a small bowl.

2 Add cream to sugar mixture and beat until stiff peaks form. Whisk in vanilla yogurt, orange juice and vanilla until smooth. Fold in mandarin oranges, reserving a few pieces for the top for garnish.

3 Spoon yogurt mousse into serving dishes and garnish with remaining orange sugar and mandarins.

ORANGE CANDIED PECAN GARNISH

In a small skillet, bring 3 tbsp (45 mL) orange juice and 3 tbsp (45 mL) granulated sugar to boil until starting to turn golden. Stir in 1/2 cup (125 mL) pecan halves and cook, stirring over low heat for about 7 minutes or until mixture is fragrant and pecans are well coated. Spread onto parchment paper to cool completely. Break up and sprinkle over top of yogurt mousse, if desired.

MANGO COCONUT ORANGE ICE POPS

MAKES 5 TO 6 ICED TREATS · · · ·

Enjoy a delicious dairy-free frozen treat when temperatures are hot. We love the creamy texture and flavor that the coconut provides.

2 cups (500 mL) chopped ripe mango

1 cup (250 mL) coconut milk

3 tbsp (45 mL) orange juice concentrate

1/2 tsp (2 mL) vanilla

Pinch salt

1. In a blender, combine mango, coconut milk, orange juice concentrate, vanilla and salt. Blend until smooth, then pour into molds, insert treat sticks and freeze at least 8 hours or overnight.

TIP

The ice pop mixture will expand when frozen, so remember to not overfill molds.

SMALL-BATCH STRAWBERRY RASPBERRY ICE POPS

MAKES 4 ICED TREATS · · · ·

Here's a cool, quick and easy way to enjoy berries. You can make a fun icy beverage by placing an ice pop into a glass and adding sparkling water. Serve right away. For an alcoholic cocktail version, try a sweet white wine, sparkling rosé, prosecco or champagne.

3 cups (750 mL) sliced strawberries

1 cup (250 mL) raspberries

1/4 cup (60 mL) strawberry jam

1 tbsp (15 mL) lemon juice

Pinch salt

1. In a blender, combine strawberries, raspberries, jam, lemon juice and salt. Blend until smooth, then pour into molds, insert treat sticks and freeze at least 8 hours or overnight.

TIP

Ice pops can also be frozen in any small container that has a smooth interior such as paper cups, plastic cups, silicone cups or small drinking glasses. If using an alternative mold, you'll need to hold the treat stick in place with foil or plastic wrap.

COFFEE GRANITA

SERVES 4 TO 6 · 🍳 5 · 🍳 · 🌿

Crunchy flakes of cold, sweetened coffee, with or without a
dollop of whipped cream, makes a refreshing summer's eve
dessert. You can also enjoy this treat as a drink by buzzing it up
in the blender with cream. (See Coffee Granita Blend, below.)
Sit back and watch the sunset while sipping away.

4 cups (1 L) hot espresso or
strong coffee

½ cup (125 mL) granulated
sugar

1 cinnamon stick

1 cup (250 mL) whipped
cream (optional)

1 In a shallow metal 13- by 9-inch (33 by 23 cm) baking
pan, combine hot coffee, sugar and cinnamon stick.
Stir to dissolve sugar and place in refrigerator until
cold. Remove cinnamon stick.

2 Place pan in freezer for about 1 hour or until crystals
begin to form around edges of pan. With a fork, stir
crystals into center of mixture. Return to freezer
and continue stirring every 30 minutes until liquid is
frozen and mixture looks granular, about 3 hours.

3 Serve in large goblets and dollop with whipped
cream, if desired.

COFFEE GRANITA BLEND

Scoop half of the frozen coffee granita into
blender and add 1½ cups (375 mL) table (18%)
cream. Blend until smooth. Pour into tall glasses
and serve. Repeat with remaining frozen granita
and another 1½ cups (375 mL) table (18%) cream.
You can use half-and-half (10 %) cream or milk if
desired. Serves 4 to 8.

TIP

If you like your coffee sweet, add up to another
¼ cup (60 mL) of granulated sugar to the
hot coffee.

NO-BAKE BISCOFF ICEBOX CAKE

SERVES 8 TO 10 ·

This is the perfect make ahead potluck and party dessert. An impressive, easy-to-make sweet, it uses Biscoff cookies that are sandwiched between layers of whipped cream that has just a hint of coffee and spice. After refrigeration, the cookies soften and transform to a cakelike texture. It's the kind of dessert that might have you standing in front of the fridge with spoon in hand.

CAKE

2 cups (500 mL) heavy or whipping (35%) cream

1/4 cup (60 mL) confectioners' (icing) sugar

2 tsp (10 mL) instant coffee granules

1/2 tsp (2 mL) ground cinnamon

1/8 tsp (0.5 mL) ground cloves

2 packages (8 oz/250 g each) Biscoff or Speculoos cookies

TOPPING

1 1/2 cups (375 mL) heavy or whipping (35%) cream

1 tbsp (15 mL) confectioners' (icing) sugar

1 tsp (5 mL) vanilla

Prepared caramel sauce

Toffee bits

1 Line an 8- by 4-inch (20 by 10 cm) loaf pan with plastic wrap; set aside.

2 CAKE: In a large bowl, whip cream, sugar, coffee granules, cinnamon and cloves to medium-soft peaks. Spread a thin layer of cream into bottom of prepared pan to help hold first layer of cookies in place. Spread one side of the cookies with about 1 tbsp (15 mL) cream mixture, then stack upright, on their sides, in the pan in rows that line up along the length of the pan. Continue, making a second layer of cookies on top. Spread any remaining cream over top. Lay remaining cookies flat on top of pan; you may need to break a few cookies to make them fit. Cover with plastic wrap and refrigerate for at least 6 hours or overnight.

3 TOPPING: Half an hour before serving, prepare topping. In a bowl, whip cream and sugar to firm peaks. Turn the cake out onto a serving platter, remove plastic wrap and cover with about half of the whipped cream. Swirl or pipe remaining whipped cream on top. Drizzle some caramel sauce on top or sprinkle with caramel bits, we like to use both!

4 Place in freezer for 15 minutes or until whipped cream firms up. Slice and plate while the cake is firm. Cover and refrigerate any leftovers.

MAKE AHEAD

Cake can be frozen for up to a month after it has chilled in the fridge. Wrap well and thaw in the refrigerator overnight; decorate as directed.

UPSIDE-DOWN GRANOLA RHUBARB CAKE

SERVES 8 TO 10 ·

This combination of tart rhubarb and an almost caramelized granola topping is divine. Use our delicious Skillet Granola (page 20) or store-bought granola for this recipe. The cake is delicious as is, but if you want to get a little fancy, serve with whipped cream or a scoop of ice cream.

TOPPING

1/4 cup (60 mL) melted butter

1/2 cup (125 mL) packed light brown sugar

1/2 cup (125 mL) granola

1 cup (250 mL) chopped fresh or frozen rhubarb

CAKE

1 1/2 (375 mL) cups all-purpose flour

3/4 cup (175 mL) granulated sugar

1/2 tsp (2 mL) ground cinnamon

1/2 tsp (2 mL) baking powder

1/4 tsp (1 mL) baking soda

1/4 tsp (1 mL) salt

1/2 cup (125 mL) butter, softened

2 large eggs

3/4 cup (175 mL) buttermilk

1 tsp (5 mL) vanilla

1 TOPPING: Preheat oven to 350°F (180°C). Spray a 9-inch (23 cm) round, 2-inch (10 cm) deep baking pan with cooking spray. Add the melted butter and brown sugar to the baking pan, stir to combine then spread evenly in pan. Evenly sprinkle the granola on top, followed by the rhubarb.

2 CAKE: In a large bowl, using a stand or handheld mixer, combine flour, sugar, cinnamon, baking powder, baking soda and salt. Add the butter and mix until texture looks sandy. Beat in eggs one at a time, scraping down sides of bowl as needed. On low speed, add half of the buttermilk; increase speed to medium and beat for 1 minute. Gradually add remaining buttermilk and vanilla and beat until well combined, about 30 seconds; set aside.

3 Spoon the batter on top so it covers the rhubarb; smooth the top. Bake for 35 to 40 minutes or until a tester inserted in the center comes out clean.

4 Let cool in pan for 5 minutes, then run a knife around the edge of the cake. Place a plate on top of the pan then flip over and let cake release from the pan while it's still warm. Don't worry if some of the granola sticks to the bottom of the pan — no one needs to know! — simply remove and place back on top of cake.

TIP

Do not thaw the frozen rhubarb before using.

MINI PHYLLO BUTTER TARTS

MAKES 24 MINI TARTS ·

Butter tarts are irresistible — and very easy to make using phyllo pastry. Mini tart or muffin tins with cups about $1\frac{3}{4}$ inches (4.5 cm) in diameter and about $\frac{3}{4}$ inch (2 cm) deep are ideal for these tiny bites.

FILLING

1 large egg

$\frac{1}{2}$ cup (125 mL) packed brown sugar

$\frac{1}{2}$ cup (125 mL) corn syrup

2 tbsp (30 mL) butter, softened

1 tsp (5 mL) vanilla or $\frac{1}{2}$ tsp (2 mL) maple extract

PHYLLO CUPS

$\frac{1}{2}$ cup (125 mL) butter, melted

5 sheets phyllo pastry

1 FILLING: In a bowl, whisk together the egg, brown sugar, corn syrup, butter and vanilla; set aside.

2 Preheat oven to 375°F (190°C). Set 24 mini muffin tin on counter.

3 PHYLLO CUPS: Arrange 1 sheet of phyllo on work surface. Keep unused phyllo layers covered with a barely damp tea towel. Brush first sheet lightly but thoroughly with butter. Cover with second sheet; brush with butter. Repeat layers, finishing with brushing the fifth layer with butter. Cut the phyllo into 24 equal pieces. Gently but firmly ease each square, buttery side up, into the mini muffin cups, pressing the pastry along the bottom and up the side. Using a spoon, divide filling evenly among phyllo cups.

4 Bake in lower third of preheated oven for about 12 minutes or until pastry is crisp and golden. Let tarts cool slightly before removing gently from pan.

TIPS

Nonstick mini tart/muffin tins make removing these tarts a snap. For regular mini tart/muffin tins, lightly grease the cups and around their rims.

Store in a single layer in shallow airtight containers for up to 3 days.

NUT VARIATION

Sprinkle bottom of each phyllo cup with some toasted walnuts or pecans. Not crazy for nuts? That's okay; you can use raisins or currants.

CARROT CAKE SANDWICH COOKIES

MAKES 10 SANDWICH COOKIES · · ·

These scrumptious soft cookie sandwiches are guaranteed to disappear quickly. The dough and the filled cookies need a little chilling time, but the short wait is worth it!

COOKIES

½ cup (125 mL) packed dark brown sugar

½ cup (125 mL) butter, softened

1 large egg

1 tsp (5 mL) vanilla

1 cup (250 mL) all-purpose flour

½ tsp each baking soda, baking powder and ground cinnamon

¼ tsp each ground nutmeg, ground ginger and salt

¾ cup (175 mL) finely grated carrot

⅓ cup (75 mL) quick oats

¼ cup (60 mL) shredded coconut

CREAM CHEESE FILLING

½ pkg (8 oz/250 g) brick-style cream cheese, softened

¼ cup (60 mL) butter, room temperature

½ tsp (2 mL) vanilla

1¼ cups (310 mL) powdered (icing) sugar

1 COOKIES: In a bowl, using an electric mixer, beat the brown sugar and butter together until well combined. Beat in egg and vanilla. Sift in flour, baking soda, baking powder, cinnamon, nutmeg, ginger and salt; stir until well combined. Add carrots, oats and coconut; stir until combined.

2 Preheat oven to 350°F (180°C). Line two baking sheets with parchment paper. Using a heaping tablespoon (15 mL) measure, drop dough onto prepared baking sheets, about 2 inches (5 cm) apart. Press each mound down a bit to flatten slightly. Bake, one sheet at a time, for 12 to 13 minutes until golden around the edges and bottoms are beginning to brown. Let cool on baking sheet for 5 minutes, then transfer to a wire rack. Cool completely.

3 FILLING: In a bowl, using an electric mixer, beat cream cheese, butter and vanilla until fluffy. Gradually beat in powdered sugar until fluffy; mixture will be soft.

4 To assemble the cookies, divide filling to place an equal-size dollop on the flat underside of half the cookies, then press the flat side of another cookie on top. Refrigerate sandwich cookies for 20 minutes before enjoying.

MAKE AHEAD

Filled cookies can be stored in the refrigerator for up to 2 days in an airtight container.

SKILLET OATMEAL CHOCOLATE CHIP COOKIE

SERVES 8 ·

Browning the butter helps create an extra decadent richness in this warm cooking. Get the ice cream ready and dig in!

1 cup (250 mL) unsalted butter, cubed

1 cup (250 mL) packed light brown sugar

1/2 cup (125 mL) granulated sugar

2 large eggs

2 tsp (10 mL) vanilla

1 1/2 cups (625 mL) all-purpose flour

1 cup (250 mL) quick oats

1 tsp (5 mL) baking soda

1/2 tsp (2 mL) baking powder

1/2 tsp (2 mL) salt

1 bag (7 oz/200 g) 70% dark chocolate chunks or dark chocolate chips

Flaky sea salt for sprinkling

1 Preheat oven to 350°F (180°C).

2 Place butter into 10-inch (25 cm) cast-iron skillet. Place over medium heat and melt butter, stirring occasionally. Once butter is melted, cook the butter, stirring milk solids off bottom and sides of the skillet constantly for 3 to 4 minutes until milk solids become golden and have a toasty aroma. Remove from heat and let stand for 10 minutes. Whisk in brown and granulated sugars until combined. Whisk in eggs, one a time, and then whisk in vanilla until mixture looks creamy.

3 In a bowl, whisk together flour, oats, baking soda, baking powder and salt.

4 Using a wooden spoon, stir flour mixture into skillet until most of the flour is absorbed. Stir chocolate until evenly distributed and no flour remains. (Chocolate will melt slightly.)

5 Bake for about 25 minutes or until light golden around edge and top is just set but still soft. Remove from oven and sprinkle with flaky salt. Let cool on a wire rack for 10 minutes before serving.

TIP

If you can't find this size bag of chocolate you can measure out 1 1/4 cups (310 mL) coarsely chopped chocolate or chips.

PEANUT BUTTER TRUFFLE SQUARES

MAKES 64 SQUARES · ·

Peanut butter and chocolate are a creamy and salty match that we adore! Creating a pan of these yummy squares can be cut into small truffle-size bites that will adorn any dessert platter for entertaining.

PEANUT BUTTER LAYER

¹⁄₄ cup (60 mL) butter, softened

¹⁄₂ cup (125 mL) packed brown sugar

¹⁄₂ cup (125 mL) smooth peanut butter (not all-natural)

1 large egg

1 cup (250 mL) all-purpose flour

¹⁄₄ tsp (1 mL) baking soda

DARK CHOCOLATE TRUFFLE FILLING

4 bars (3¹⁄₂ oz/100 g each) 72% cocoa chocolate, chopped

1 cup (250 mL) heavy or whipping (35%) cream

1 tsp (5 mL) vanilla

64 peanut halves (optional)

1 **PEANUT BUTTER LAYER:** Preheat oven to 350°F (180°C). Line a 9-inch (23 cm) square baking pan with parchment paper.

2 In a large bowl, using an electric mixer, beat butter, sugar and peanut butter until smooth. Beat in egg until well blended. Stir in flour and baking soda until well blended.

3 Spread and pat into prepared pan. Bake for about 15 minutes or until slightly soft in center and golden around edges. Let cool completely.

4 **DARK CHOCOLATE TRUFFLE FILLING:** Meanwhile, wipe out bowl and add chocolate. Heat cream and vanilla in microwave until bubbly. Pour over chocolate and let stand for 2 minutes. Whisk until melted and smooth. Pour over cooled peanut butter base and spread evenly. Refrigerate for about 2 hours or until set. Remove from pan and cut into 64 small squares. Top each square with a peanut half, if using.

TIP

Freeze these truffle squares in an airtight container for up to 1 month or refrigerate for up to 2 weeks.

SLOW COOKER PUMPKIN CRÈME BRÛLÉE

SERVES 6 · 🔲 · 🍲 · 🌿

This dessert is an elegant cousin to pumpkin pie. We love the pleasure of breaking into the caramelized sugar topping for this delicious flavor. We also love a make-ahead dessert that makes hosting easier.

1 cup (250 mL) heavy or whipping (35%) cream

1 cup (250 mL) half-and-half (10 %) cream

1/2 cup (125 mL) granulated sugar

2 large eggs

2 large egg yolks

1 tsp (5 mL) vanilla

1/4 tsp (1 mL) ground cinnamon

1/4 tsp (1 mL) finely grated nutmeg

1/8 tsp (0.5 mL) ground cloves

1/2 cup (125 mL) pumpkin purée

Granulated sugar for caramelizing

1 Use a 6- to 7-quart slow cooker for recipe. Set aside six 3/4-cup (175 mL) ramekins or small ovenproof bowls or cups.

2 In a microwave-safe bowl, whisk together creams and sugar. Heat in microwave until warm.

3 In a medium bowl, whisk together eggs, egg yolks, vanilla, cinnamon, nutmeg and cloves. Whisking constantly, gradually add warm cream until well blended, then whisk in pumpkin. Divide the mixture among the ramekins.

4 Place six ramekins in slow cooker. Carefully pour enough hot water into slow cooker to come halfway up the sides of the ramekins. Cover and cook on High for 2 to 4 hours or until set but still jiggly. Remove from slow cooker and let cool to room temperature on a wire rack. Cover and chill in the refrigerator for at least 3 hours or up to 2 days.

5 Sprinkle the top of each custard evenly with about 1 tbsp (15 mL) of granulated sugar. Use a blow torch to melt the sugar until it bubbles and turns golden brown. Chill uncovered for 30 to 60 minutes before serving.

TIP

Check to make sure your slow cooker can hold six ramekins in the bottom of the crock. If there is not enough space, place a small steam rack on top of the lower ramekins, then put remaining ramekins on top.

Library and Archives Canada Cataloguing in Publication

Title: Best of Bridge done in one : perfect recipes in one pot, pan or skillet /
text by Sylvia Kong and Emily Richards.

Other titles: Done in one

Names: Kong, Sylvia, author. | Richards, Emily, author.

Description: Includes index.

Identifiers: Canadiana 20230164145 | ISBN 9780778807124 (hardcover)

Subjects: LCSH: One-dish meals. | LCSH: Quick and easy cooking. | LCGFT: Cookbooks.

Classification: LCC TX840.O53 K66 2023 | DDC 641.82—dc23

INDEX